Expert Advisor Programming And Advanced Forex Strategies

Table of Contents

Expert Advisor Programming

Introduction

Congratulations on your personal copy of *Expert Advisor Programming and Advanced Forex Strategies.* This special book will provide you with a solid foundation of the techniques required for profiting by combining expert advisor programming with advanced forex strategies. When finished you will have a deep understanding of the forex market from several angles. The emphasis throughout is on practical applications which is the style of all my works. Thanks for choosing this book!

Basics of Trading

What is trading in financial terms?

Trading is buying or selling an instrument with the aim to profit from the trade. You speculate on the price going up or down. You can either go **long(buy)** where you buy an instrument and attempt to sell it at a higher price. Or you can go **short(sell)** where you borrow an instrument that sells at a high price and you speculate that the price will decrease, when the price has decreased you buy it back from the market and return it to the owner, a market-maker, you keep the decrease in price as profit.

You can trade leveraged or unleveraged. If your leverage is 1:200 that means for every dollar you have in your account, you have the buying power of 200 times. If you have 500 USD in account, you can buy for 200 x 500=10 000 dollars amount of the security. The margin is the amount that you are required to have in your account to use the leverage.

Different types of orders

Buy Market order: You buy the instrument at the current spot price.

Buy Limit order: If the current market price is 100, you can place a buy limit order at 95 to buy if the price goes down.

Buy Stop order: If current market price is 100 and you want to buy if it goes above 110 then you place a buy stop order at that level, and it will be triggered if the price goes above it. You can also do these type of orders on the sell side .ex. sell limit, sell stop, sell market.

Stop-loss and Take-profit

Sometimes the market moves quickly and if you are unable be in front of your computer it is possible to set exit orders for your trades. These orders are called **stop-loss** and **take-profit**. Stop-loss is an order that is triggered if your trade moves against you and ends with a loss. Take-profit is the opposite, it is how much profit you want from the market.

Automatic Trading

Why automatic trading – why develop algorithms of your trading strategy?

There are several advantages of quantitative trading. People have feelings and emotions attached to their money, they prefer to lose small and win big. Let us imagine you have just executed a trade, what you will experience is that you don't want to close a losing trade, it's difficult to take the loss. However, if you are in profit you will prefer to close your trade with a small profit. What you may also experience is that after closing the winning trade the market continues in your favor. It is difficult emotionally to follow the rule *"cut your losses and let profits run"*. By automating your strategy, you allow your algorithm to do the trading and detach your feelings from the strategy. You have predefined rules in your algorithm which are executed without your interaction.

As humans, it is difficult and time consuming to monitor all the markets and wait for all entry signals. By automating your trading you save time and increase the number of instruments you are able to trade because you run your algorithm on them instead. You can trade whenever you want, whichever market you want, without using so much time in front of the computer.

When you are trying to develop a trading strategy, several ideas come in your head. You start studying charts and look 2-3 months in the past to see how the strategy would have done. That period is not enough, you need to run many years of backtest to prove if a strategy is good. That can only be done by developing an algorithm and do backtesting of several years, on different instruments and timeframes. However, you don't have time to do it manually because it's time consuming and time used for developing a new trading system will decrease. By learning to code you become equipped to develop new trading strategies and you also will be able to detect false ones.

Progamming language

There are several languages you can use to program your trading strategy. What is true is that there is not much difference between the languages. If you can code one language you can code other languages too, you just need to do some tweaks in how you code, but the basics are similar for many of them.

We will use the Meta Trader 4 platform. They use mql programming which is similar to java/C/C#/C++. The reason we are using this platform are several. It's open source which means it's free to code a strategy, backtest and run it on a demo account. The trading community using this language is huge, so if you any problems you can just google the solution on the internet. You don't have to gather historical data either, it's already on the platform. Finally, many brokers are using the platform so it's not difficult to find a broker with the preferences you require.

The goal of this book is to be hands-on and it will teach you what you need to code your own trading strategy.

MetaTrader and MetaEditor

MetaTrader

MetaTrader is the platform where you trade, you have your charts, run your algorithms, test strategies, basically everything you execute is done on this platform. Here you can also do your manual trading. Everything that you normally can do on a trading platform can you do here.

3-1 Picture above shows the Meta trader.

MetaEditor

We need to launch our MetaEditor, which is a platform where you create your own indicators, algorithms which are expert advisors or write a script by coding it. You use MetaTrader to execute what you code in MetaEditor.

Open MetaTrader – go to the terminal – click on the "yellow book" – you will then open MetaEditor

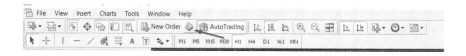

3-2 Above is picture of the toolbar on Metatrader, click on the "yellow book" which is metaEditor.

Short key is: *Alt +F4*

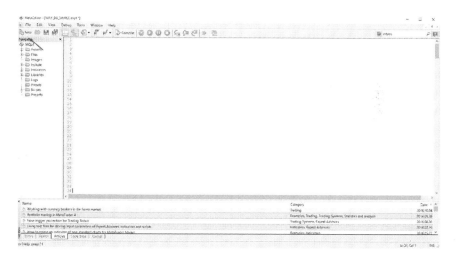

3-3 Picture shows the MetaEditor.

MetaEditor, like MetaTrader also has a toolbar which consist of buttons you frequently use.

Create new Expert Advisor/Algorithm

At the toolbar to the left you have a button called *New*, click on it.

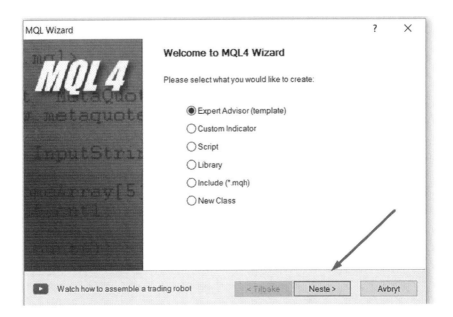

3-4 This box will appear when you click on the new button (næste=next on English platforms).

In this editor, you have an option to develop several scripts which you can run, but what we will use is Expert Advisor which is a trading Algorithm, and we tick off *Expert Advisor (template)* and press *next*. Then a wizard will appear up where you must specify the general properties of your Algorithm.

Name: You write the name of your Algorithm

Author: Who is the owner of this algorithm, write your name here

Link: If you have a website you can paste a link to it here

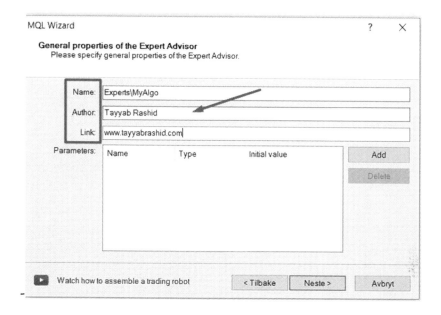

3-5 General properties wizard.

You don't need to fill in anything other than general properties, let everything else remain as is and press next.

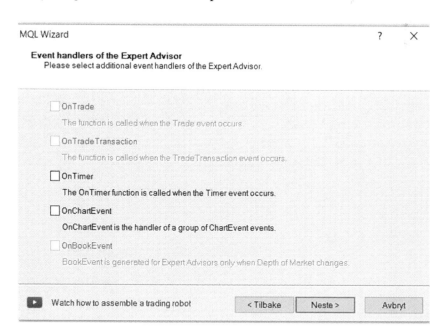

3-6 In the next window tick all the boxes and press next.

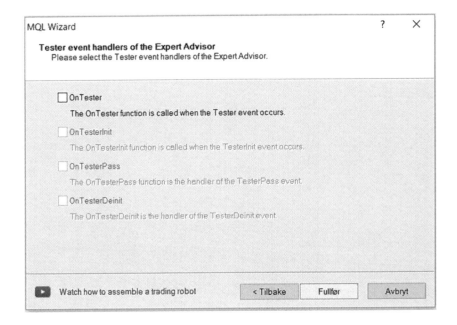

3-7 Also in next window tick all the boxes and press finish(fullfør=finish on English platforms)

Understanding of script

After finishing the *new expert advisor wizard* we should have created a skull of our first script of our algorithm. We will use this section to explain the illustration 3-8, you can see the script. Begin by examining the script carefully, everything within it, even every dot. Because everything in it has some meaning, and it's sensitive, if you write something wrong you will be unable to run it.

```
WA5_BB_SIMPLE.mq4 *   MyAlgo.mq4                        Compiles the currently open file, F7
4 //|                                                   www.tayyabrashid.com  |
5 //+--------------------------------------1-----------------------------------+
6 #property copyright "Tayyab Rashid"
7 #property link       "www.tayyabrashid.com"
8 #property version    "1.00"
9 #property strict                          2
10 //+--------------------------------------------------------------------------+
11 //| Expert initialization function                                           |
12 //+--------------------------------------------------------------------------+
13 int OnInit()
14   {
15 //---
16   6                                       3
17 //---
18    return(INIT_SUCCEEDED);
19   }
20 //+--------------------------------------------------------------------------+
21 //| Expert deinitialization function                                         |
22 //+--------------------------------------------------------------------------+
23 void OnDeinit(const int reason)
24   {
25 //---
26                                           4
27   }
28 //+--------------------------------------------------------------------------+
29 //| Expert tick function                                                     |
30 //+--------------------------------------------------------------------------+
31 void OnTick()
32   {
33 //---
34                                           5
35   }
36 //+--------------------------------------------------------------------------+
37
```

3-8 Empty skull or template of an algorithm (expert advisor).

This whole section is called a script; *this is your algorithm skull.*

1. *MyAlgo,* the name you wrote in you wizard. In editor every panel will be an algorithm and each will have its own name.

2. This section, will have everything else you wrote in the wizard, your name, author name and stating that this script is the author's property.

3. A script is built of several functions, and all the functions will be executed when you run your script on a live account or in the strategy tester. You make functions, in the functions you code what you want to do and give inputs. The function takes

your input, does the operations you have coded into it and then gives an output that you have told it to give. A function executes all operations in it. As predefined, all scripts comes with three functions, and only these three functions will be used to call on all other functions (functions can call on other functions). You can have the operation in one function that it calls on another function. As you can see on your script you will have three functions. The first is called *int OnInit()* this function will be executed when we begin using this algo, whether we place it on the chart or we use it in the strategy tester. It will be called on only once in the start. This is an expert initialization function.

4. *Void OnDeinit()* this function will be called on at the end, when we detach our algorithm from the chart or stop the strategy tester. This is an expert deinitialization function.

5. The last function to be defined is our tick function. This function is run on every tick, this means every time a trade is executed in the market. So one tick represents one trade.

6. Every line has its own number in the script so it's easy for you to track any errors. It's important to note that when you are writing, the first instruction will be executed first, then the next one and so on.

Compiler button

Compiler button runs your script and checks for errors, if it has errors it will let you know and you should fix them. Press the compiler button to check for any errors, and check if your algorithm works. Always press compiler button as you code your algorithm to check for errors. If you check for errors at the end it can be difficult to fix so many errors at once. Under the script you will get a new box, if there are no errors it will give an output of 0 errors. It also shows how much time it took to run thru the script, in the box it shows that it took 1407 Milliseconds to run this empty script. If you are trading high frequency it's important to code effectively so that you can decrease the time it takes to run your script.

3-9 At the bottom you will get an error messages if something is wrong with your script.

Introducing Flowcharts

What is a Flowchart?

When you are coding or programming, you are writing a program which consist of different functions and you make a logic where the different functions are executed one after the other. To understand the logic of a script sometimes it's better to use flowcharts, which we will use in the remainder of the book.

A common definition of a Flowchart:

*A **flowchart** is a type of diagram that represents an algorithm, workflow or process, showing the steps as boxes of various kinds, and their order by connecting them with arrows. This diagrammatic representation illustrates a solution model to a given problem. Flowcharts are used in analyzing, designing, documenting or managing a process or program in various fields.*

A script can either run in real-time on a demo or a live account, then you must attach your algorithm to a chart or test in the strategy tester. Under the development of an algorithm you might use the strategy tester frequently and test your algorithm, then run it on your account. In our development, we will only use strategy tester to test our script.

Objects of a flowchart

Shape	Name	Description
→	Flowline	An arrow coming from one symbol and ending at another symbol represents that control passes to the symbol the arrow points to. The line for the arrow can be solid or dashed. The meaning of the arrow with dashed line may differ from one flowchart to another and can be defined in the legend
(stadium shape)	Terminal	Represented as circles, ovals, stadiums or rounded (fillet) rectangles. They usually contain the word "Start" or "End", or another phrase signaling the start or end of a process, such as "submit inquiry" or "receive product".
(rectangle)	Process	Represented as rectangles. This shape is used to show that something is performed. Examples: "Add 1 to X", "replace identified part", "save

		changes", etc...
	Decision	Represented as a diamond (rhombus) showing where a decision is necessary, commonly a Yes/No question or True/False test. The conditional symbol is peculiar in that it has two arrows coming out of it, usually from the bottom point and right point, one corresponding to Yes or True, and one corresponding to No or False. (The arrows should always be labeled.) More than two arrows can be used, but this is normally a clear indicator that a complex decision is being taken, in which case it may need to be broken-down further or replaced with the "predefined process" symbol. Decision can also help in the filtering of data.
	Input/Output	Represented as a parallelogram.

		Involves receiving data and displaying processed data. Can only move from input to output and not vice versa. Examples: Get X from the user; display X.
	Predefined	Represented as rectangles with double-struck vertical edges; these are used to show complex processing steps which may be detailed in a separate flowchart. Example: process-files. One subroutine may have multiple distinct entry points or exit flows (see coroutine). If so, these are shown as labeled 'wells' in the rectangle, and control arrows connect to these 'wells'.
	Preparation	Represented as a hexagon. May also be called initialization. Shows operations which have no effect other than preparing a value

		for a subsequent conditional or decision step. Alternatively, this shape is used to replace the Decision Shape in the case of conditional looping.
⬭	On-page connecter	Generally represented with a circle, showing where multiple control flows converge in a single exit flow. It will have more than one arrow coming into it, but only one going out. In simple cases, one may simply have an arrow point to another arrow instead. These are useful to represent an _iterative_ process (what in Computer Science is called a _loop_). A loop may, for example, consist of a connector where control first enters, processing steps, a conditional with one arrow exiting the loop, and one going back to the connector. For additional clarity,

		wherever two lines accidentally cross in the drawing, one of them may be drawn with a small semicircle over the other, showing that no connection is intended.

4-1 Explanation of the elements in a flowchart.

Flowchart of a simple algorithm template

We begin by making a flowchart of the template we created in the last chapter with the predefined functions and see how things work.

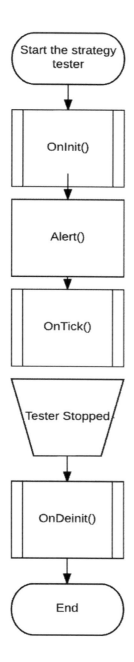

4-2 Flow chart of the simple algorithm template from last chapter.

Explanation of Flow chart in illustration 4-2

1. It starts by you clicking the strategy tester, pressing the button on your platform.

2. Then it executes everything stated in the OnInit() function, it will only execute once.

3. When the initialization function is finished, it is also finished with everything in the OnInit() function. Then it calls the OnTick() function which runs every time a new tick occurs, when a new trade in that instrument has been made. It will continue running this function until the strategy tester is finished(either manually by us or it has run thru all the sample periods).

4. You can stop the strategy tester manually by pressing the *stop* button, or when the run is finished for the time period this will automatically stop it. Please note the shape of the flowchart object, this is the shape of manual operations. So when this event happens it will stop running the script and execute the next operation.

5. When we have stopped the strategy tester, everything in OnDeinit() function will be executed. We have reached the end of the algorithm and our script is finished.

By now you should understand the flow of the predefined functions in our skull. It starts from the top of the flowchart and executes all. After it's finished executing everything in a function, it passes control to the next operation in our flowchart.

Exercise

Try to delete OnDeinit() from the script and then compile. Does it have any impact on the error? Did you get any errors that you have to include in that function?

Introducing Functions

What is a function?

Coding is about you designing different functions; you have input into the function and you want it to do something. You can either get an outcome of the function or you could just simply use it to do something like place a trade.

An output function looks like this:

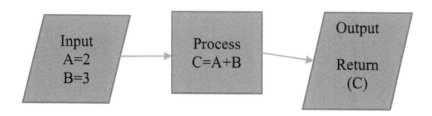

5-1 Illustration of a function that has an output.

You have input variables and assign a value to them. In the process, you add both input values and get a new variable C which holds the added value, which is the output from this function. When you execute this function it will return variable C, which in this case holds a value of 5.

Non-output function look like this:

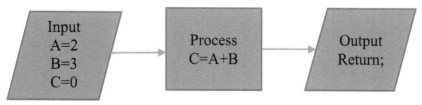

5-1 Illustration of a function which has no output.

This is the other type of function, here you have three variables as inputs A, B and C. They have values assigned to them 2,3 and 0. Also in this we have a process which is adding A+B and assign this added value to variable C. When the process is finished, C will hold the value of 5(A+B = 2+3) and the function will return nothing, and both are called functions. It just gives a new value to our variable C and returns nothing.

Defining input variables

You can use words and numbers in the function. You must always begin with defining which type of variable it is, name the variable, and then assign the value you want to use in your function.

Let us say you want to make a function that adds 2+3 and we get an answer. If we just write 2+3= this is incorrect, you will get an error message and it will not run.

You begin by defining your input variables. Whole numbers like 2 and 3 are an *integer(int)* type of variable.

You write these input variables like this:

```
int A=2;
int B=3;
int C=0;
```
5-3

All three are integer type of variables, so they begin with the word *int*, a space, and then we write our variable. We want to name that value, our value 2 is named A. So in the process when you want to use the number 2, you use it by writing variable names like C=A+B.

You should also note the semicolon at the end of each variable. Assigning value to each of the variables is a separate operation, and we end each of the operations with a semicolon. Above we have three operations, when the program is reading our script after the semicolon, it knows that one operation is finished. It assigns its value and goes to the next operation, assigning value to the next variable. *We will use a semicolon every time an operation is finished.* It's like a period in a sentence.

Different types of variables in Mql4

Integer: This variable is whole numbers meaning 1,2,3,4
Example:

```
int ShortMA=20;
int LongMA=100;
```

5-4

We have declared variables which can be input variables for different moving average periods in a moving average function. Note the semicolon again.

Double: This is a variable which is a number with a decimal 1.02, 0.02, etc

Example:

```
double Stoploss=0.0020;
```

5-5

String: Is a text type and must always be written with quotes like "Hedge", "Martigale" or "EURUSD"

Example:

```
string word="helloword";
```

5-6

Bool: This is a variable which can have value of TRUE or FALSE, it's Boolean type

Example:

```
bool yes=TRUE;
```

5-7

Exercise:

Define which type of variable is:

John, 1.2, 50, 100, and Your Trading System

Types of a function

The types of functions are decided by what outcome you want from them. We can begin by dividing functions in two main groups based on whether they give an output or not.

Output functions type

Integer: Same as input variable, if you are making a function where the output is an integer this is the type of function.

Double: Same as double input variable, if your output is going to have decimals you need this type of function.

String: Same as string input variable, if your output is going to be text type this is your function type.

Boolean: Same as Boolean input variable, if your output is going to either stating false or true its Boolean type.

What they all have in common is that they return something back.

Non-output function type

There is only one type and it's called **void**. This is a function which only executes what is in the function but doesn't give output, it returns nothing. Mostly it's used to calculate another variable we have defined but not assigned a value to as yet, or to execute another function.

Objects of a function

```
functiontype FunctionName()
{

return;
}
```

5-9

Figure 5-9 shows objects of a function.

Functiontype: Which can be int, double, string or bool if it's output function or void if it's non-output function.

FunctionName: Here you will write the name of your function followed by an opening and closing parentheses (). Also look that we have finished a line but this time we are not ending the line with semicolon, this is because we are not finished with this process yet. Like a line alone, this function type and function name doesn't make sense.

Opening and Closing brackets: All the function must be on the line after defining the type and giving the name ending with parentheses. The next line should be opening bracket { that signals the start of the function. Everything you write after the bracket, the following lines will be executed when you call on this function. We close the function with a closing bracket } to define a end of the function, but before the end we have to write *return;* if it's *void* type and *return(what we want to return)* if it's an output function.

Task 1: Make a function where you have three input variables A, B and C.

A=3

B=4

C=0

Where the function will add A+B and assign the value to C, then C should be the input variable and Name it MyFunction.

```
int MyFunction()
{
    int A=3;
    int B=4;
    int C=0;

    C=A+B;
    return(C);

}
```
5-10

Above you can see an output function, since we have an output type integer which is a whole number, the function type is int. Then we give it the name MyFunction(), and set an opening bracket. Then we define all the variables we will use, they are integer type, we end them with semicolons. After giving C the added value, we return C, which means that whenever we call on the function by writing: MyFunction(); equals value 7 which is the return value.

Task 2:

Make a function where you have three input variables A, B and C.

A=3

B=4

C=0

Where the function will add A+B and assign the value to C, then use function Print to Print C and Name it MyFunction.

```
void MyFunction()
{
    int A=3;
    int B=4;
    int C=0;

    C=A+B;
    Print(C);

}
```
5-11

We have the same operation in this function but the difference is the type, the aim of the function, it will not return anything. It will just print the value of the C in Terminal Journal. When you call on MyFunction(); now it will return nothing.

"Hello World" Alerts

Let us play a bit with this so that we get an understanding of how functions work and run our algorithm for the first time. Let us write an operation.

Alert("Hello World");

Alert() is a function in metatrader.

"Hello Word" is the sentence we want displayed, the sentence must be written with quotes. At the end of the operation we indicate that this operation has ended and we close the statement with semicolon ";". Let us see the help file for that function. *You highlight "Alert" and press F1*

Alert

Displays a message in a separate window.

```
void  Alert(
   argument,        // first value
   ...              // other values
   );
```

This function displays message in a separate window.

So we write this function first in OnInit() function and press compile. Like this:

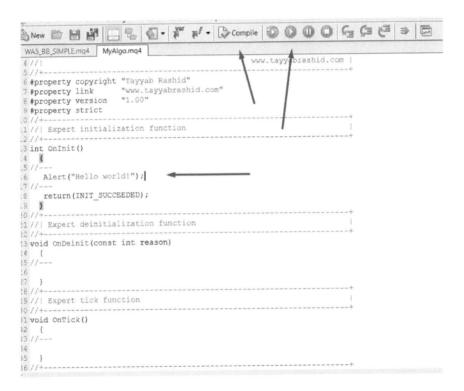

After pressing compile and we get no errors. Then we go to our Metatrader and attempt to run the script.

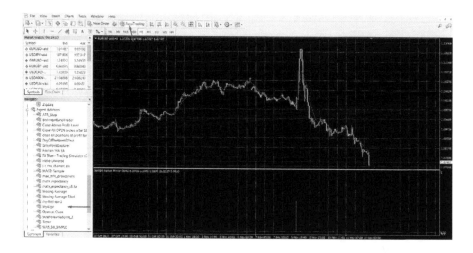

5-12 Go to the terminal enable AutoTrading and drag and drop MyAlgo on your chart.

We must first enable automate trading and then go to our navigator window in the left and drag "MyAlgo" and drop on the chart.

Next window will pop up, just click "OK".

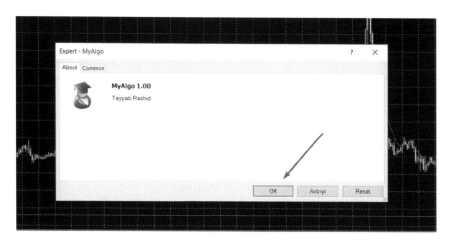

5-12 Just Click on OK.

Now the algorithm is running on this chart and timeframe. Right after you will get Alert, it's because we had the Alert() function in the

Initialization(OnInit()) function and this is run once at the start of your algorithm.

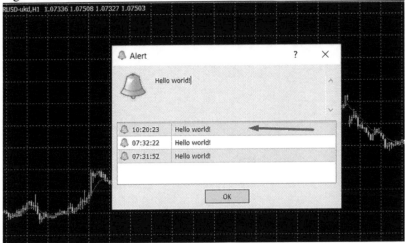

5-13 This is how the Alert will be displayed on your terminal.

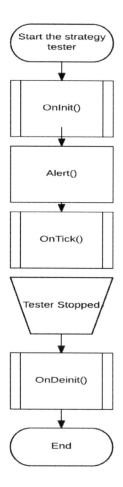

5-14 Flowchart when we have the Alert() function in the OnInit()

You see how the flows progresses, after start, it calls on the OnInit() function which calls on the Alert() function. After executing the Alert() function it then passes control to Ontick() function.

Let us experiment, now put the Alert() function in the Deinitialization function, then compile and drop again on the chart.

First we must remove the Algorithm from the chart. Right click on the chart and open the dropdown menu. Click Expert Advisor - Remove

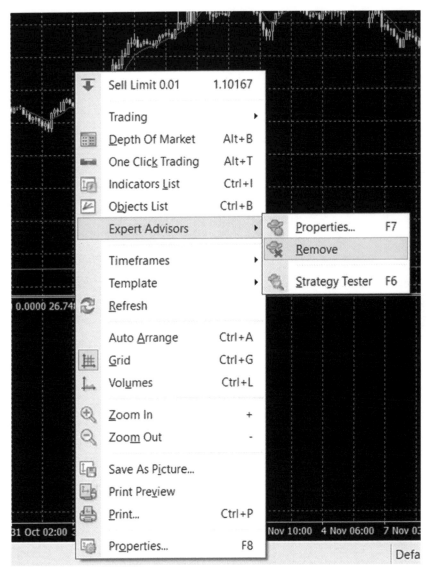

5-15 How you remove your algorithm from the chart or to stop it.

```
WA5_BB_SIMPLE.mq4   MyAlgo.mq4
 4 //|                                      www.tayyabrashid.com |
 5 //+---------------------------------------------------------------+
 6 #property copyright "Tayyab Rashid"
 7 #property link       "www.tayyabrashid.com"
 8 #property version    "1.00"
 9 #property strict
10 //+---------------------------------------------------------------+
11 //| Expert initialization function                                |
12 //+---------------------------------------------------------------+
13 int OnInit()        ◄────────────
14   {
15 //---
16
17 //---
18    return(INIT_SUCCEEDED);
19   }
20 //+---------------------------------------------------------------+
21 //| Expert deinitialization function                              |
22 //+---------------------------------------------------------------+
23 void OnDeinit(const int reason) ◄────────
24   {
25 //---
26    Alert("Hello world!");
27   }
28 //+---------------------------------------------------------------+
29 //| Expert tick function                                          |
30 //+---------------------------------------------------------------+
31 void OnTick()
32   {
33 //---
34
35   }
36 //+---------------------------------------------------------------+
```

5-16 If we put the Alert() function in OnDeinit() functio

Here we have moved our function from OnInit() to OnDeinit(). Again we drag and drop, nothing will happen, but if you now try to remove your algo from your chart, the Alert will come up. Because all functions in OnDeinit will run the function when we stop our algorithm. See diagram 5-17.

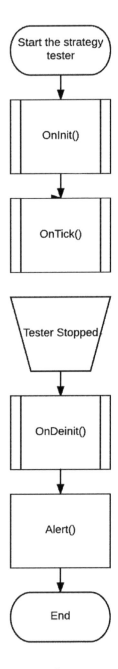

5-17 Flowchart if you put Alert() function in OnDeinit() function.

Let us put our Alert function in the OnTick() function, this runs the function on every tick. You will get messages all the time, until you stop the tester or remove the algorithm from the chart,

```
WA5_BB_SIMPLE.mq4 | MyAlgo.mq4 |
 7 #property link        "www.tayyabrashid.com"
 8 #property version    "1.00"
 9 #property strict
10 //+-----------------------------------------------+
11 //| Expert initialization function                |
12 //+-----------------------------------------------+
13 int OnInit()
14   {
15 //---
16
17 //---
18    return(INIT_SUCCEEDED);
19   }
20 //+-----------------------------------------------+
21 //| Expert deinitialization function              |
22 //+-----------------------------------------------+
23 void OnDeinit(const int reason)
24   {
25 //---
26
27   }
28 //+-----------------------------------------------+
29 //| Expert tick function                          |
30 //+-----------------------------------------------+
31 void OnTick()
32   {
33 //---
34    Alert("Hello world!");
35   }
36 //+-----------------------------------------------+
```

5-20 This is how we will put the Alert() function in the OnTick() function. We call a function by naming the function with parentheses, an input and ending it with semicolon.

The tick function will call on the Alert() function on every tick, every time a new trade has happened.

After compiling your algorithm, you drag your algo from the navigator windows and drop it on the chart again. You will now see that the Alert function is called frequently on every tick on your screen.

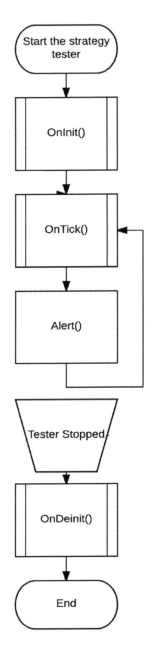

5-19 Flowchart when you put Alert() function in the OnTick() function.

What you should know now.
- How to begin writing a script – New Algo
- OnInit(), OnDeinit() and Ontick() functions
- How to compile your algo
- How to run your Algo
- How to stop your running Algo
- How to display an Alert

Declare different input variables

There are two places. One of the places is called global area, the variables declared here can be used in any of the other functions, and this area is above all the functions, above the OnInit() function also.

5-20 How we declare input variables in the global area.

1. To declare an integer variable we use *int,* it's important to note

that this programming language is case sensitive so if you write *INT or Int* you will get an error message. You see that when we write int the correct way we get that word in blue but when we write Int we get that word in black, which is incorrect. Next, which is important, you see in line 13 that we don't have a semicolon after the statement, this mean we haven't closed this statement, then it's another error.

So four takeaways from this:

1. int= this is an integer type of variable
2. Name of the variable is *ShortMA*
3. The value assigned to this variable is 20
4. We close every stand alone statement with a semicolon;

2. We use *double* to tell which type of variable this is, this is a variable with a numeric value that includes decimals, and we assign a value to it.

3. We use *string* to tell which type of variable this is, name of the variable is a *word* and then we assign "HelloWorld" as value, *remember* the quotes and we add and close this operation or statement with a semicolon.

4. All these variables are declared above all other functions, this is key because then we can use them in all the functions below. This program executes the first statement first and then below. So, if you have a function on line 5 but the variable used in the function is on line 15, then this function will not have a variable to use because it's not declared. *All these variables are declared outside of any function, this means all of them can be used in any functions below, but if we declared a variable within a function we can only use that variable in that particular function.*

Last in the picture above you can see that the last variable has *extern* written in front of it. This is because now we can change this variable when we are testing the strategy(running this algorithm) and we can optimize it.

In the script above if you delete lines 13 and 17 and then compile you will get no errors and you can run your script. Then drag and drop this algo on any chart and you will get a box, click on the panel called *input*, you will see that only the variable where we have *extern* before it can be changed. Therefore, if you use a variable that you want to be changeable you simply need to write *extern* before it.

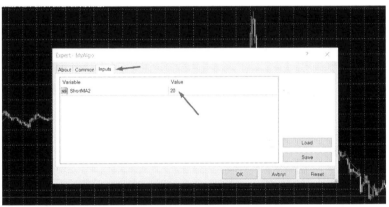

5-21 Input box when you use extern variables.

Picture 5-21 illustrates how we use local variables, those variables are declared within the function and can only be used by this function.

```
void MyFunction()
{
    int A=3;
    int B=4;
    int C=0;

    C=A+B;
    Print(C);

}
```

5-21 This shows how the input variables appear in the local area.

We use *global variable* when we want to change the input variable later when we are running the strategy or optimizing it. It can be used in the global area when there are several functions using the same input variable. Maybe you have designed a function where you assign value to a variable using function one, and then a variable with an assigned value by function one is used by function two.

What you should know from this session:
- Different types of variables used, string, integer and double
- How to declare a variable
- How to end a statement or operation
- That this programming language is case sensitive must write right letter
- Where in the script variables should be declared
- How to declare changeable variables

NewOrder() Function

Description of the function

We are going to make a function called NewOrder() this will be a void type of function, and returns nothing. Remember for *void* we have to write it in lower case.

Creating the function

```
void NewOrder()
{
return;
}
```

6-1 We start by writing void, Name of the function, opening and closing bracket.

This is the start of writing the function, we have not written anything in it yet, it's an empty skull. It is opening and closing of the function. The type is void because this function will not return anything, name is NewOrder followed by opening and closing parentheses. On next line we have an opening bracket and then write *return;* before the closing bracket of the function.

```
WA5_BB_SIMPLE.mq4    MyAlgo.mq4 *
12 //| Expert initialization function                        |
13 //+----------------------------------------------------------+
14 int OnInit()
15   {
16 //---
17
18 //---
19    return(INIT_SUCCEEDED);
20   }
21 //+----------------------------------------------------------+
22 //| Expert deinitialization function                        |
23 //+----------------------------------------------------------+
24 void OnDeinit(const int reason)
25   {
26 //---
27
28   }
29 //+----------------------------------------------------------+
30 //| Expert tick function                                    |
31 //+----------------------------------------------------------+
32 void OnTick()
33   {
34 //---
35
36   }
37 //+----------------------------------------------------------+
38 //+----------------------------------------------------------+
39 //|Our own New order send function                          |
40 //+----------------------------------------------------------+
41 void NewOrder()
42 {
43 return;
44 }
```

6-3 The new function is below all the other functions, the predefined functions.

It's important to know that all the functions we build will be written below our predefined functions in the script.

We will now make a function which has the following input variables in the global area:

extern double TakeProfit=0.0050

extern double StopLoss=0.0025

extern double LotSize=0.01

All of them have extern which means they can be changed when we are running this strategy or in the strategy tester.

OrderSend()

This is an integer type of function. Which returns a value of 1 if the market order has opened and a negative value if the market order was not opened successfully.

int Result=OrderSend(); *We have a storing variable called Result which will store the value this function is returning.*

OrderSend() function has some input variables, which you separated by comma.

1. Symbol, this one we will write as Symbol() because this function will return the symbol of the chart this algorithm is running on

2. Order type we have 6 different order types
   a. OP_BUY=Market buy order
   b. OP_SELL=Market Sell order
   c. OP_BUYLIMIT=Buy limit order
   d. OP_BUYSTOP =Buy stop order
   e. OP_SELLLIMIT=Sell limit order
   f. OP_SELLSTOP=Sell stop order

3. Amount or lotsize since we can either write lotsize directly here or have a variable which we have assigned a lotsize amount to and write it instead.

4. Price can be either ask or bid. Since we want to buy we use the current ask price. We will never get our order filled at bid price if we want to buy. Just try to use bid and you will not get any trades filled if buying.

5. Slippage, how much slippage do we allow, meaning what can be the difference between the price we see as bid and the actual

price we get for our order. We will set it to 3 pips.

6. Stoploss, if we set it as 0, we will not have any stop loss. We can either write a value right into this field our assign value to a variable and write the variable instead. We have already assigned a value to our variable StopLoss so we will use that instead. Because this a buy order we have to subtract stoploss from the ask price, and that price level will be our stop loss.

7. Same as Stoploss, we will use a Takeprofit variable. But with buy orders we must add takeprofit to the ask price, to get our take profit level.

8. Comment, if we want any comment to be displayed we write it as a string with quotes or NULL if we don't want any comment. We have used NULL here.

9. Magicnumber: We use 1234. This is not anything special but you might have a different magicnumber if you are running several algorithms on the same pair.

10. This variable is expiration time, when you want this order to be cancelled, if you set it to 0, it will never be cancelled. This variable is in seconds.

11. Arrow, if you want to mark any arrow on the chart when this trade executes you write it here, but we don't want it so we write just clrNONE.

By now you should have finished your OrderSend() function and closed with a closing parentheses and semicolon, you should have this function:

```
void NewOrder()
{
    int
Result=OrderSend(Symbol(),OP_BUY,LotSize,Bid,3,StopLo
ss,TakeProfit,NULL,1234,0,clrNONE);
return;
}
```

6-4 Our first NewOrder() function is finished.

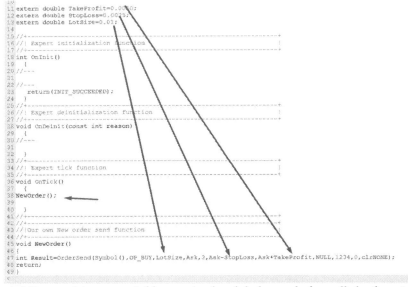

6-5 External input variables are in the global area before all the functions even predefined ones.

You see that all variables are declared in the beginning, the function is below all three predefined functions.

The variables are defined above all the functions and they are used in the function. We use the name of the variables rather than the values themselves in our function. The OrderSend() function ends with semicolon because this operation is finished, then as we close the whole function with return;. You can see that we call on the function NewOrder(), which calls on OrderSend() with all of our input parameters.

Now you just have to call on this function NewOrder(), this is done by writing NewOrder() in our tick function. Because every time a new tick comes in, all things stated in tick function will be run. Let us place this new function here, remember these functions also need to end with semicolon to close this operation. See line 38. You call a function by writing the name of the function with opening and closing parentheses followed by a semicolon. As shown in the next picture:

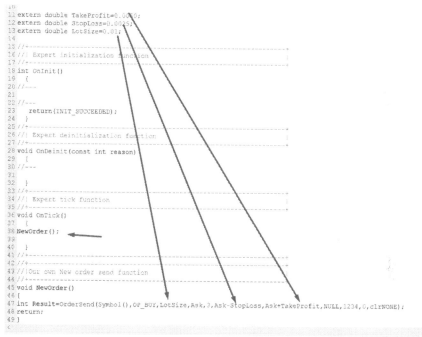

```
10
11 extern double TakeProfit=0.0050;
12 extern double StopLoss=0.8025;
13 extern double LotSize=0.01;
14
15 //+--------------------------------------------------+
16 //| Expert initialization function
17 //+--------------------------------------------------+
18 int OnInit()
19   {
20 //-----
21
22 //---
23     return(INIT_SUCCEEDED);
24   }
25 //+--------------------------------------------------+
26 //| Expert deinitialization function
27 //+--------------------------------------------------+
28 void OnDeinit(const int reason)
29   {
30 //---
31
32   }
33 //+--------------------------------------------------+
34 //| Expert tick function
35 //+--------------------------------------------------+
36 void OnTick()
37   {
38 NewOrder();
39   }
40
41 //+--------------------------------------------------+
42 //+--------------------------------------------------+
43 //|Our own New order send function
44 //+--------------------------------------------------+
45 void NewOrder()
46 {
47 int Result=OrderSend(Symbol(),OP_BUY,LotSize,Ask,3,Ask-StopLoss,Ask+TakeProfit,NULL,1234,0,clrNONE);
48 return;
49 }
```

6-6 How our Neworder() function is used in the tick function

Now you can compile this file.

Press F4 – to open the platform

Press Ctrl+R – to open the strategytester

Now choose MyAlgo file, run on EURUSD, on Tickdata and the timeframe you want.

Because you are running the NewOrder() function in the Tick() function it will place a new order on every tick, so it's going to be many orders. You can see in the flowchart below that after it has placed an order it gives again control to the OnTick() function which calls on the NewOrder() function until the tester has stopped. Congrats! You have now run your first script.

What you should know:

- How to build a function
- How to run on strategy tester

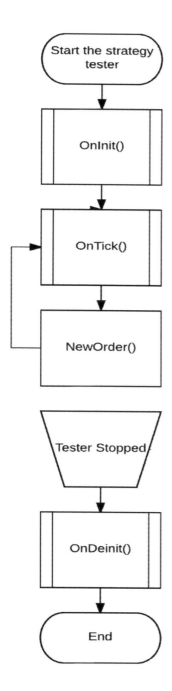

6-7 Flowchart with NewOrder() function.

IsNewBar function

The problem with the previous function is that it sends new orders on every tick, so let us make a function which checks whether a new tick also represents new bar or this tick belongs to the same bar as the previous. We need to check this because we only want to run our strategy once on each bar.

Function description

We will design a Boolean function that will return true if there is a new candle on the chart and return false if there isn't a new candle. It will check this on every tick used in the tick function before the NewOrder() function.

Function description: This function will be checked on every tick and on every tick this function will return TRUE if it's a new candle and FALSE if it's the same candle.

Function name: IsNewCandle()

```
bool IsNewCandle()
{
    static int BarsOnChart=0;
    if(Bars==BarsOnChart)
    return(false);
    BarsOnChart = Bars;
    return(true);
}
```

7-1 This is the full function IsNewCandle().

We will make a flowchart which explains this function.

1. We begin by writing type which is a bool(because it will return false/true) and the name of the function which is IsNewCandle(), then an opening and closing bracket.

2. We declare a variable static int BarOnChart=0; which stores the number of bars on the chart. This variable will be static, meaning that when this function is executed on every tick it

will store the number of bars. This is to ensure that the next time we run this function we will compare the number of bars on the chart with the last time we executed it.

3. We use an if-statement which is a decision-making statement. We ask if the bars on the chart on this particular tick are the same as the last time, we store the number of bars. As mentioned, we do this by using an if-statement and equal sign (==). By using function *Bars* this returns the numbers of bars since we started running this algorithm.

4. Independent of whether it's true or false, we assign the number of bars to our BarsOnChart variable.

5. If the bars on the chart has changed, the if-statement is answered with no, we return true;

6. If the bars on chart have not changed, the if-statement is answered with no, this function returns false.

Until we get a tick which is part of a new candle this function will return false. If you are running a one hour timeframe and this candle is a part of new hour it will return true.

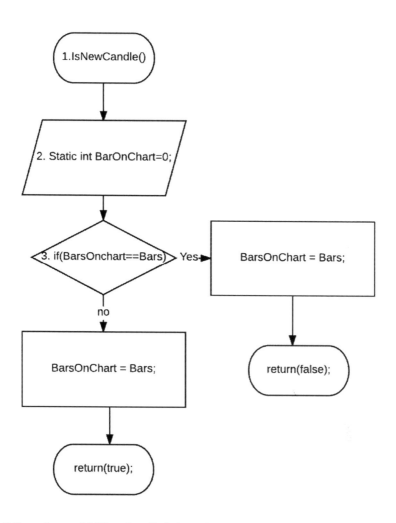

7-2 flow chart of IsNewCandle() function.

```
//+--------------------------------------------------------------+
//|Our own New order send function                               |
//+--------------------------------------------------------------+
void NewOrder()
{
int Result=OrderSend(Symbol(),OP_BUY,LotSize,Ask,3,Ask-StopLoss,Ask+TakeProfit,NULL,1234,0,clrNONE);
return;
}

bool IsNewCandle()
{
    static int BarsOnChart=0;
    if(Bars==BarsOnChart)
    return(false);
    BarsOnChart = Bars;
    return(true);
}
```

7-3 Here you can see our latest function under our previous function in the script.

How to use IsNewCandle() function

The aim of this new candle function is to only trade once per candle, this means we will put our NewOrder() function within the brackets of the if(IsNewCandle) statement

7-4 You can see how we change the flow of the Ontick function, we rearranged it.

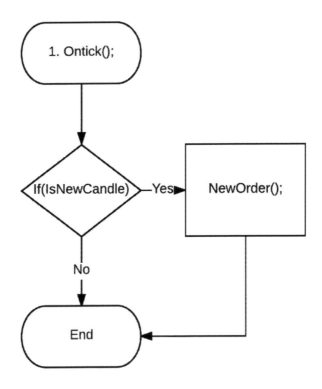

7-4 Rearranged ontick function with IsNewCandle().

You can see that we have changed the OnTick() function. We

have added an if-statement which runs the NewOrder() function only if there is a new candle.

You can see that when the Ontick() function executes, it executes if-statement which runs the function IsNewCandle(), if is NewCandle() returns true, it means yes it will execute the NewOrder() function, but if IsNewCandle() returns false it will just go to the end of the new function, and run the same way on the next tick.

What you should know:

-   How to make a bool function
-   What bars functions means
-   If statement, how we use this

Total Orders Function

Function description

This function counts the number of market orders we have in the market. The goal is to know how many open orders we have to prevent opening more than one market order at a time.

Function name: TotalOpenTrader()

```
int TotalOpenOrders()
{
int Trades=0;
int Total=OrdersTotal();
    for(int i=Total;i>0;i--)
            {
            bool res=OrderSelect(i-
1,SELECT_BY_POS,MODE_TRADES);
            if(OrderType()==OP_BUY || Order-
Type()==OP_SELL)
                {
                Trades++;
                }
        }
        return(Trades);
}
```

8-1 This is how the function looks.

Since this will return a whole number which is the number of orders this is an integer type of function.

1. We start by declaring a variable int Trades and assign a value of zero, this is the variable we will assign the number of open trades to.

2. We begin another function which is also integer type, we assign value of OrdersTotal() to *Total*, this function returns the total open and pending orders in our open trade pool.

3. We create a for loop. This is a loop which will iterate the

number of all pending orders and open orders if the number is above zero, and it will decrease the value of i after each loop, as long as i is greater than or equal to zero.

4. Next it will check if the value of i is above zero, if there are any orders in the terminal it will be above zero, like 2.

5. If we don't have any orders in the terminal it will just execute Return(Trades); which will return 0, and pass the control outside of this function.

6. If i is above zero it will run thru the rest of the loop.

7. First process is to select the particular order in our trade pool. We do this by using our OrderSelect() function, this function will return true if there is a trade in our open trade or else false. If the statement with OrderSelect() combined has two operations in our function, one is to select the right order and since it is a boolean type return of the function, it will return true which then passes control to the next operation. OrderSelect has three variables, first variable is index of the trade we are running thru the loop, we must set i-1, because the first trade has an index value of zero. The next variable we use indicates that we select the trade by its position in the index. Then we tell it that we want to use the live trade pool, not to select historical trades. OrderSelect() is a Boolean type of variable which returns true if we have any trades selected and false if no trades are selected.

8. Then we have an if-statement, which checks whether the trade we have selected is a buy or sell market order.

9. If it's a buy or sell order we add 1 to our variable Trades, if not

it will just pass control back to for loop to decrease i. If we have 8 total orders in the pool, next time i will have the value of 7 in the loop.

10. When it has run thru all open orders i will have a value of 0, and then the control will be passed to return(Trades) which return Trades variable to whom may be calling on this function. So if there are 7 market orders, variable Trades will have a value of 7 when we return(Trades) outside the function.

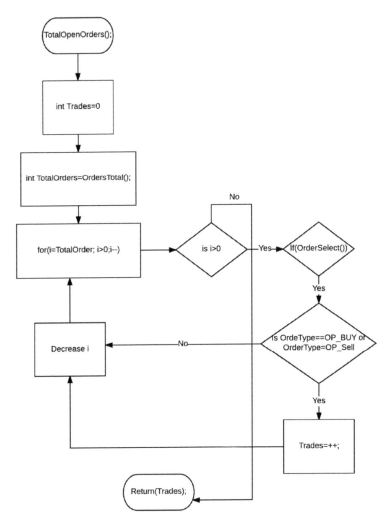

8-2 Flow chart for the TotalOpenOrders().

How to use TotalOpenOrder() function

We will now use our new function in our tick function to check and only trade if there are no open orders, meaning if TotalOpenOrder()<1.

```
25 //+------------------------------------------------+
26 //| Expert deinitialization function               |
27 //+------------------------------------------------+
28 void OnDeinit(const int reason)
29   {
30 //---
31
32   }
33 //+------------------------------------------------+
34 //| Expert tick function                           |
35 //+------------------------------------------------+
36 void OnTick()
37   {
38   if(IsNewCandle())
39     {
40       if(TotalOpenOrders()<1)
41         {
42         NewOrder();
43         }
44     }
45   }
46 //+------------------------------------------------+
47 //+------------------------------------------------+
48 //| Our own New order send function                |
49 //+------------------------------------------------+
50 void NewOrder()
51 {
52 int Result=OrderSend(Symbol(),OP_BUY,LotSize,Ask,3,Ask-StopLoss,Ask+TakeProfit,NULL,1234,0,clrNONE);
53 return;
54 }
```

8-3 *This is our rearranged OnTick() function.*

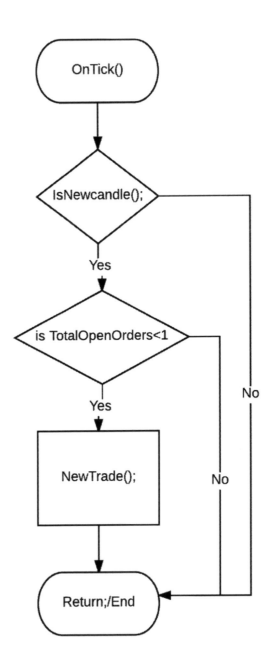

8-4 Flowchart of the rearranged Tick function.

This is how the flow runs, if it's NewCandle it will pass the control to check if total open orders is less than one meaning zero, if that's the case it will pass control to NewTrade() and execute that function NewTrade() function.

You see that we have introduced a new if-statement in our OnTick() function and now we have an additional open and closing bracket. Therefore NewTrade() is within the brackets of TotalOpenTraders statements which is within the IsNewCandle opening and closing brackets. You see the relationship in the flowchart.

Close All Orders Function

Function description:

We will make a function that closes all market orders and delete all current pending orders.

Function name: CloseAllOrder()

```
void CloseAllOrders()//1.
{
int Total=OrdersTotal(); //2.
   for(int i=Total;i>0;i--) //3.
       {
         if(OrderSelect(i-1,SE-
LECT_BY_POS,MODE_TRADES))//4.
           {
             if(OrderType()==OP_SELL)//5.
               {
                 bool res1=OrderClose(OrderTicket(),Order-
Lots(),Ask,3,clrNONE);//6.
               }
             if(OrderType()==OP_BUY)//7.
               {
                 bool res2= OrderClose(OrderTicket(),Order-
Lots(),Bid,3,clrNONE);//8.
               }
             if(OrderType()==OP_BUYLIMIT || Order-
Type()==OP_BUYSTOP|| OrderType()==OP_SELLSTOP||Order-
Type()==OP_SELLLIMIT)//9.
               {
                 bool res3= OrderDelete(Order-
Ticket(),clrNONE);//10.
               }
           }
       }
return;
}
```

9-1 This is the CloseAllOrder function.

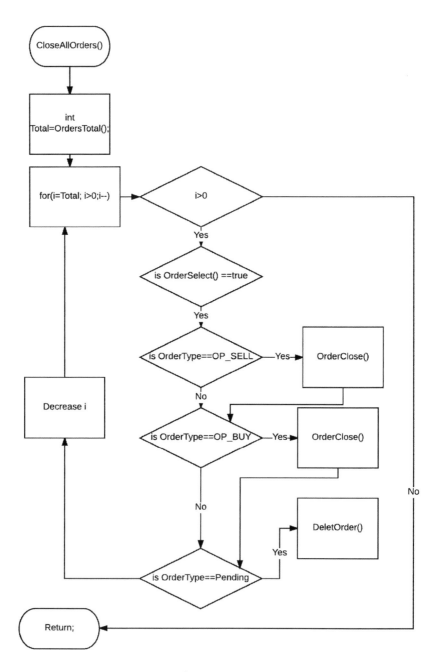

9-2 Flowchart for CloseAllOrder() function.

See the numbers marked in the function and read the comments.

1. We start by writing void + function name + adding open and close brackets and writing return;. Before the closing bracket we will include the rest of the function between the brackets and before the return; statement.

2. Create integer variable name Total, OrdersTotal() function will return the number of total current market and pending orders.

3. Create a for loop which will loop all the orders thru the loop, beginning with the last order. It will need its own opening and closing brackets, everything we want to loop must be within these brackets. If it is a total of 8 orders, it will start by the last number, 8, and run this particular order thru everything we have in our loop. After it is finished it will take order number 7 and continue until order number 1.

4. We use our OrderSelect() function to select the particular order in our order pool, for ex. we have 8 orders, order number 8 will have index number 7 in the pool. It will return true if an order is selected, if there is no order in order pool it will not run this loop, so this if-statement will always be true.

5. This will check if the selected ordertype is a market order and is a sell order, by using OrderType() function which will return ordertype. If that's the case is it will execute the next operation, which is CloseOrder().

6. We have a semicolon, because this is the end of this loop, OrderClose returns a TRUE/FALSE statement so we use bool res1 to store this value, same with the OrderDelete() function,

it will also return true. This function has three input variables.

7.
   a. First variable is OrderTicket() of the selected order
   b. Second variable is the amount you want to close, meaning OrderLots()
   c. Third is the price, since the selected order is sell order we use Ask as the closing price
   d. Fourth variable is slippage we set it to three pips
   e. Comment

8. This will check if the selected order is a market order, if it is a buy order it will execute the next operation.

9. We have semicolon, because this is the end of this loop, we close with the bid price because this is a buy order.

10. This will check whether the selected order is pending or not.

11. We use OrderDelete() to delete this particular order if it's a limit order.

Use of CloseAllOrder() function

This function will be used by another function which is CandleClose() function which we will create later in the book.

Pips Function

Description of the function

Some brokers are four digits others are five digits. This means some are denoting prices in 1.5000, other brokers are denoting prices in 1.50000. You need a function that retrieves 0.0001 if it's four digits and 0.00001 if it's a five. I need a variable double pip, which I want to assign 0.0001 value to. The point is to have a variable that you can multiply with an integer variable to convert that to pips, for example, use it in deciding the stop loss and take profit.

You have an external integer variable called extern int Stoploss=50;

It's an integer variable stating that the stoploss should be 50 pips. When you are applying this variable you want it to be 0.0050 which is 50 pips. You can do this by having a variable called pips that you assign a value of 0.0001 to it. You can then multiply Stoploss*pips=50*0.0001=0.0050 and get the value you want to use in your function.

This function should only run once in the beginning when we start our algorithm in our OnInit() function and assign a new value to our *double pips* variable in the global area.

```
void PipsFunction()//1.
{
double
ticksize=MarketInfo(Symbol(),MODE_TICKSIZE);//2.
    if (ticksize == 0.00001 || ticksize == 0.001)//3.
    {
    pips = ticksize*10;//4.
    }
    else
    {
    pips = ticksize;//5.
    }
return;
}
```

10-1 This is the PipFunction.

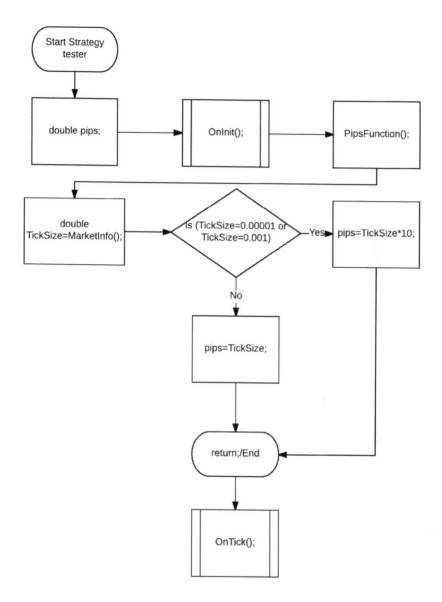

10-2 Flowchart for PipsFunction;

Comment to the function:
You see that first we begin the strategy tester, which then defines the variable double pips, and it gets no value because we will use PipsFunction() to assign value to it. Then control passes to the OnInit()

function which calls on the PipsFunction();

1. We start by defining the function, it's a void function with the name PipsFunction() and we add an opening and closing brackets with return; before the closing bracket in the end. This is a function that only executes and returns nothing.

2. We have a double variable TickSize, which equals MarketInfo(Symbol(),MODE_TICKSIZE); we close this operation with a semicolon. MarketInfo() function, retrieves information from the market, which if it's a five digit broker it will retrieve 0.00001 and if it's four digit broker it will retrieve 0.0001 for example on EURUSD pair.

3. Then we have an if-statement which checks whether or not the broker is five digits. If in the last operation it retrieved a value of 0.00001 (TickSize), this is a five digit broker. Then we multiply TickSize with 10 and assign the value to our variable pips: If the TickSize is 0.0001 this means it's a four digits broker then we just use the same value to pips, and there is no need for multiplying it because it already holds the value 0.0001.

4. If it is a five digit broker, we multiply by 10 to convert it to four digits, and assign this value to the pips variable.

5. If it's a four digits broker and the four digit broker pips is the same as market info view retrieved pips=ticksize. This is an else statement if the first is not true, then we execute this operation else not.

```
 7 #property link        "www.tayyabrashid.com"
 8 #property version    "1.00"
 9 #property strict
10
11 extern double TakeProfit=0.0050;
12 extern double StopLoss=0.0025;
13 extern double LotSize=0.01;
14 double pips=0;    ◄─────────
15 //+--------------------------------------------------+
16 //| Expert initialization function                   |
17 //+--------------------------------------------------+
18 int OnInit()
19   {
20 //---
21    PipsFunction();    ◄─────────────
22 //---
23    return(INIT_SUCCEEDED);
24   }
25 //+--------------------------------------------------+
26 //| Expert deinitialization function                 |
27 //+--------------------------------------------------+
28 void OnDeinit(const int reason)
29   {
30 //---
31
32   }
33 //+--------------------------------------------------+
34 //| Expert tick function                             |
35 //+--------------------------------------------------+
36 void OnTick()
37   {
38    if(IsNewCandle())
39      {
40        if(TotalOpenOrders()<1)
41          {
42            NewOrder();
43          }
44      }
45   }
46 //+--
```

10-3 This is how we will use PipsFunction in the script.

You see that the pips variable are defined in the global area because they can be used in several different functions.

We run this function only once therefore we put it in OnInit(). Remember it runs only at the start, so we run it and assign value to our pips variable which we can use in all other variables in the operation. For example, before we begin, our variable pips have no value. When we start the strategy tester, execute the algorithm and when the OnInit() function has been completed it will execute the PipsFunction(); which assigns value to our *pips* variable.

We are building the different functions that we need to manage our trades. What we now need are the following functions: trade, trade execute, lotsize, break-even, and the trailing stop.

BreakEven Function

Description of the function

Name of The function: BreakEven()

This function will run and check after a predefined distance whether the market has moved in our favor and lock in some pips.

This function will only run if we have an open order, it runs on every tick and not the candle close. We will use the if-statement to check whether there is an open trade, and call this function in tick function if a trade is open. We will have a true/false variable which we put in the OnTick() function to turn breakeven function on/off, and have this variable as changeable in our global area.

Variables in global area:

Extern int MoveToBreakEven=50; This variable we will use to decide after how many pips in our favor that we want to change to break-even.

Extern int PipsProfitLock=20; This variable is used to decide how many pips we want to secure in profit, 0 means break-even and 20 pips means we want to lock in 20 pips of profit.

Extern bool UseBreakeven=true; This variable we use in the tick function, and runs break-even and if this variable is true, it can be changed in the input window.

```
void BreakEven()//1.
{
for(int i=OrdersTotal();i>0;i--)//2.
    {
    if(OrderSelect(i-1,SELECT_BY_POS,MODE_TRADES))//3.
    {
        if(OrderType()==OP_BUY)//4.
            {
            if(Bid-OrderOpenPrice()>MoveToBreakE-
ven*pips)//5.
                {
                if(OrderOpenPrice()>OrderStopLoss())//6.
                    {
                    bool res1=OrderModify(OrderTicket(),Or-
derOpenPrice(),OrderOpenPrice()+PipsProfit-
Lock*pips,OrderTakeProfit(),0,clrNONE);//7.
                    Alert("Yes");
                    }
                }
            }
        if(OrderType()==OP_SELL)

            {
            if(OrderOpenPrice()-Bid>MoveToBreakE-
ven*pips)
                {
                if(OrderOpenPrice()<OrderStopLoss())
                    {
                    bool res1=OrderModify(Order-
Ticket(),OrderOpenPrice(),OrderOpenPrice()-PipsProf-
itLock*pips,OrderTakeProfit(),0,clrNONE);
                    }
                }
            }
        }
    }
}
```

11-1 Breakeven function.

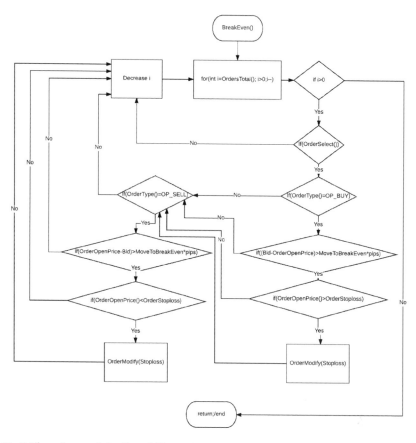

11-2 Flowchart of the BreakEven function.

1. We start by naming the function void BreakEven(), add the open and close brackets and write return before our close bracket.

2. We will use a for loop to loop thru all open orders thru our breakeven function. i equals TotalOrder() and will return current total orders, then begin running the loop thru the latest order. If there are 8 orders it will begin with the eighth order and decrease order number for every time it has looped thru the function. It will run if i is greater than 0, if i equal 0 it will then pass the control to the end of this function.

3. We use OrderSelect() to select a particular order in our trade pool, as long as there is an order in the pool it will return true else false. If the last decision making passes to OrderSelect() this means there is an order in our trade pool, so this will always be true, and passes control onward after selecting the order.

4. After we have Orderselected() and it has returned true, we check if the selected order is a buy order. If it is a buy order, it will pass the control to the next operation, if not it will run thru the rest of the function which checks if this is a sell order.

5. If it's a buy order the statement will check if the difference(in pips) between current price and order opening price is more than what we have decided in the extern variable MoveToBreakEven . For example if we have set that variable to 40, that variable is not in pips, for us to convert it into pips we multiply with our pips variable which is (0.0001), this will become 0.0040. If the difference is more than 0.0040, the market has moved more than 40 pips in our favor, this will pass the control to the next operation. If it's not true it will then run the same order thru the sell operation which is also in the function further down.

6. This if statement will check whether the stoploss has already moved by breakeven or trailing function if it has not moved before. This will return true, and it will pass to the next operation. Else pass control to check if it's a sell order and run that operation.

7. Then we use OrderModify() function to execute what we want it to do, everything else is same as the initial order, what we want to change is the stoploss. Since it's a buy order we have

to add pips we want to lock in to the OrderOpenPrice(), here again PipsProfitLock is a numeric value like 20 to convert it to pips by multiplying with our pips variable.

8. Then we do the same for the sell side. You see that both orderType() functions are within OrderSelect() function's brackets.

```
11 extern int TakeProfit=50;
12 extern int StopLoss=25;
13 extern double LotSize=0.01;
14 double pips;
15 extern int MoveToBreakEven=50;
16 extern int PipsProfitLock=20;
17 extern bool UseBreakEven=True;
18 //+------------------------------------------------+
19 //| Expert initialization function                 |
20 //+------------------------------------------------+
21 int OnInit()
22   {
23 //---
24   PipsFunction();
25   Alert(pips);
26 //---
27    return(INIT_SUCCEEDED);
28   }
```

11-3 This is how the variable will be in the global area.

In the picture above, we have included variable double pips, we have not assigned any value to it but we have a defined double function. To assign value to it we call on the PipsFunction() at initialization. We have also changed TakeProfit and Stoploss to integer type because instead of 0.0025 we have written 25, on the other side have we multiplied StopLoss and Takeprofit by pips to convert it to 0.0025. We have also used NomalizeDouble() function to convert all to have four decimals in order to round to four decimals.

```
void NewOrder()
{
int
Result=OrderSend(Symbol(),OP_BUY,LotSize,Ask,3,Normal
izeDouble(Ask-
StopLoss*pips,4),NormalizeDouble(Ask+TakeProfit*pips,
4),NULL,1234,0,clrNONE);
return;
}
```

11-4 New order function.

How we use BreakEven Function

We will use it in our Ontick function and before we run the breakeven function we need to check if there is an open order, if there is then it will execute the breakeven function on every tick.

```
void OnTick()
  {
  if(IsNewCandle())
      {
        if(TotalOpenOrders()<1)
            {
            EntrySignal();
            }
      }
      if(TotalOpenOrders()>0)
            {
            if(UseBreakEven)
                {
                BreakEven();
                }
            }
  }
```

11-5 BreakEven function included in the OnTick Function.

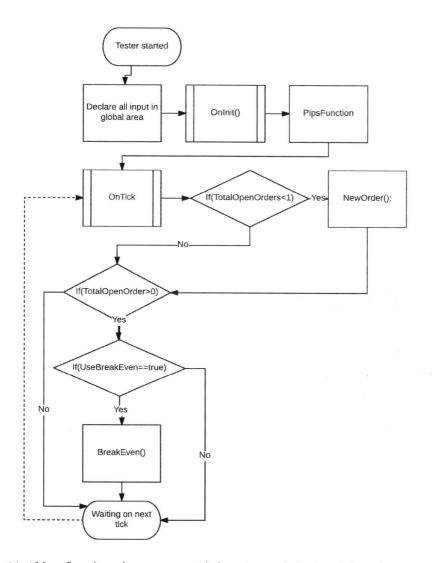

11-6 New flowchart from start to tick function with the BreakEven function included.

You see that in the OnTick() function after executing a trade it will have TotalOpenOrder, if more than one, it passes control to the next if-statement which asks if we have set the UseBreakEven to true, if that's the case it will pass control to the next operation which is running the BreakEven() function.

Trailing Stop Function

Description of the function

Function name: TrailingStop() this is also a void function.

We want to trail our stoploss in an uptrend, we trail some(distance) pips below the bid, for example 50 pips below the current bid price. After our trailing stop is triggered if the market moves up 50 pips we will change our stop loss 50 pips on the upside.

Variables used in the global area:

Extern bool UseTrailingStop=true; This variable is called on in the tick function, as our BreakEven() function and checks whether we want to use a trailing stop, after the trade has been triggered.

Extern int WhenToTrail=50; We use this variable to see if the market has moved more than this amount of pips when we begin the trailing stop. If we are long and the market has moved in our favor 50 pips we begin trailing the stop loss.

Extern int TrailAmount=50; This variable is what distance we want between our new stop loss and the recent bid price. 50 means we want to trail 50 pips below the recent price. We must multiply both of these with pips to convert these number to pips, 0.0050.

```
  void TrailingStop()//1.
{
   for(int i=OrdersTotal();i>0;i--)//2.
      {
      if(OrderSelect(i-
1,SELECT_BY_POS,MODE_TRADES))//3.
         {
         if(OrderType()==OP_BUY)//4.
            {
            if(Bid-
OrderOpenPrice()>WhenToTrail*pips)//5.
               {
               if(OrderStopLoss()<Bid-
TrailAmount*pips)//6.
                  {
                  bool
res1=OrderModify(OrderTicket(),OrderOpenPrice(),Bid-
TrailAmount*pips,OrderTakeProfit(),0,clrNONE);//7.
                  }

               }
            }
         if(OrderType()==OP_SELL)
            {
            if(OrderOpenPrice()-Bid>WhenToTrail*pips)
               {
if(OrderStopLoss()>Bid+TrailAmount*pips)
                  {
                  bool
res1=OrderModify(OrderTicket(),OrderOpenPrice(),Bid+T
railAmount*pips,OrderTakeProfit(),0,clrNONE);
                  }
               }
            }
         }

      }
return;
}
```

12-1 Trailingstop function.

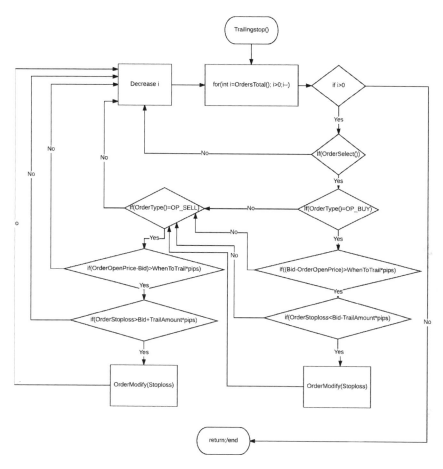

12-2 Flowchart of the TrailingStop() function

1. We start by defining the function void TrailingStop() with an open and closing bracket, and return; before the closing bracket.

2. Here we run all the open orders thru our loop of statements. We use a for loop to do that. Starting with the latest and decrease *i* for each time the loop has been executed until *i* is zero, then it will pass the control out of this function.

3. We select our order by using OrderSelect() the function has

the same input as before. If an order is selected and there is an order in our order pool it will be true. It will have the selected order and pass the operation to the next statement. This will always be yes because if there is no order it will not begin the loop because then TotalOrder() equals 0, which passes control directly out of the loop.

4. With this if-statement operation we check whether the selected order is a buy order, if so, this statement will pass the operation to the next one or else it will run the same order thru the sell operations which are further down, after which it will begin the loop again with the next order.

5. This if-statement checks whether the difference between the current and open price is more than the number of pips we have decided we want to trail after with the WhenToTrail variable. We multiply this variable by pips to convert from 40 to 0.0040. If our variable is 40, the market has moved more than 40 pips in our favor, this statement will pass the operation to the next statement or else it will pass control to check if this is a sell order.

6. This checks if this is a buy order, if our current stop loss is less then where we want to trail. If orderstoploss is 1.4500 and we want the trail stop loss to be at 1.4505 then this statement will become true and pass operation to the next statement, meaning we must change the stop loss to where we want to trail. Otherwise it will pass control to check if this is a sell order and run thru the remainder of those operations.

7. We Use OrderModify() function to change stoploss behind the bid price we want stoploss to trail, we also use pips to convert TrailAmount to pips.

Declaration of variables in Global Area:

```
extern int TakeProfit=50;
extern int StopLoss=25;
extern double LotSize=0.01;

double pips;

extern bool UseBreakEven=True;
extern int MoveToBreakEven=50;
extern int PipsProfitLock=20;

extern bool UseTrailingStop=true;
extern int WhenToTrail=50;
extern int TrailAmount=30;
```

12-3 This is the global variable area with the trailingstop function.

How to use TrailingStop

As a BreakEven() function this will also be placed in our OnTick function after TotalOpenOrders>0 if- statements.

```
void OnTick()
  {
  if(IsNewCandle())
     {
      if(TotalOpenOrders()<1)
         {
         EntrySignal();
         }
     }
     if(TotalOpenOrders()>0)
         {
         if(UseBreakEven)
            {
            BreakEven();
            }
         if(UseTrailingStop)
            {
            TrailingStop();
            }
         }
  }
```

12-4 This is the OnTick() function when you include the TrailingStop function.

As with the BreakEven() function we include this function in the same brackets, within brackets of the if-statement checking if there is an open order. If orders are open it will check if we have set Usebreakeven to true, if that's true it will run the breakeven function. It then checks if we have set UseTrailingStop to true, if that's the case it will run the Trailingstop function. If we have no open orders it will go to the end of the program.

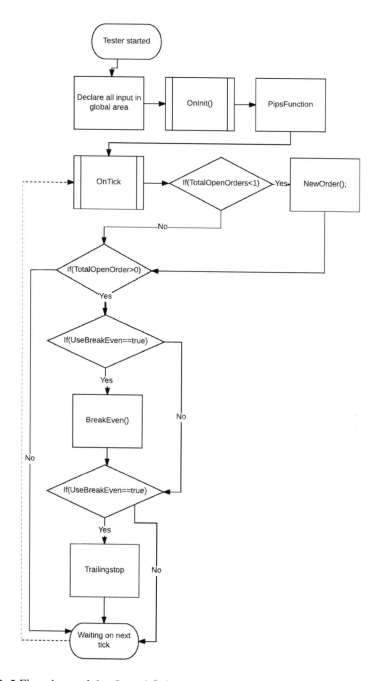

12-5 Flowchart of the Ontick() function with the TrailingStop included

Trade Function

Description of the function

We have been making functions, the most important is the trade sending function, which includes the option to turn stoploss and takeprofit off, set takeprofit as a function of stoploss(risk/reward) and the option to positionsize.

Function name will be: Trade(int direction)

Int direction is an input parameter which we will use to call if we want to trade a buy or sell order.

Trade(0) for buyorder and Trade(1) for sellorder.

We will have the option to have a stop loss or no stop loss.

We will have the option to have a take profit or no take profit.

We will have a position with a risk/reward ratio, for this we need the stop loss turned on.

We will have automated position sizing, this needs the stop loss turned on and be able to choose risk percent per trade.

Variable in Global Area:

extern bool UseStoploss=true; This will be true if want to use stop loss and false if not

extern bool UseTakeProfit=true; This will be true if we want to use takeprofit, false if not

extern bool UsePosition=true; This will be true if we want to use positionsizing, false if not extern bool UseRiskReward=true; This will be true if we want to use Risk/reward ratio

extern double reward_ratio=2; This is the risk reward ratio, if it's true this means takeprofit is double of stoploss

extern int RiskPercent=1; This is positionsizing percent how many percent of our current equity do we want to trade on each trade, our risk on each trade.

Call on the function:
This function will be called by a trade Logic function which we will define by Trade(0) or Trade(1).

```
void Trade(int Direction)//1.
{
double SL;//2.
double TP;//3.
double Equity=AccountEquity();//4
double RiskedAmount=Equity*RiskPercent*0.01;//5.
double Lots=0;//6.
   if(Direction==0)//.7
   {
   if(UseStoploss)//8.
      {
      SL=Bid-StopLoss*pips;
      }
      else
      {
      SL=0;
      }
     double PipsToBuyStoploss=StopLoss*pips;
     if(UseTakeProfit)//.9
        {
        if(UseRiskReward && UseStoploss)//10.
           {
           TP=(Bid-SL)*2+Bid;
           }
        else
           {
           TP=Bid+TakeProfit*pips;
           }
        }
        else
        {
        TP=0;
        }
     if(UsePosition && UseStoploss)//.11
     {
      Lots=(RiskedAmount/(Pip-
sToBuyStoploss/pips))/10;
     }
     else
     {
     Lots=LotSize;
     }
```

13-1 Trade() function.

1. This function is a void function. We write void Trade(int direction), open and closing brackets and return before the

closing bracket to tell the executor that this is the end of this function and the control will be given outside the function from there. Direction is an input variable that will be used to call on the function, it's an integer type. It will be called like Trade(0) for buy order and Trade(1) for sell order, 0 1 is integer type therefore variable Direction is a integer type.

2. We are defining a new double variable SL(stop loss) which we will use to place in our OrderSend() function with no initial value assigned to it.

3. We are defining new double variable TP(take profit) which we will use to place in our OrderSend() function with no initial value assigned.

4. We have a double function named equity, this variable will be assigned the current account value

5. We have a double variable named risked amount, this is the amount we want to risk on a particular trade. We multiply current equity with the risk we want to put on this trade with RiskPercent variable in our global area, because it's integer type and we want to convert it to percent we multiply this with 0.01

6. We have a variable called Lots, with zero initial value assigned. All these variables are local variables, they can only be used within this function.

7. When calling on the function we have called in This was Trade(0) it will run everything within this statement bracket.

8. First thing is to decide the stop loss, if UseStoploss is equal to

stoploss is Bid-Stoploss*pips else is equal to zero.

9. We decide the stop loss. If stoploss is equal to true then we have to ask whether we are using risk to reward(is this true).

10. If this is true takeprofit is for example two times stoploss if it's not true stoploss is Bid+TakeProfit*pips.

11. Then we must see if UsePosition and stoploss are equal to true, if so then lotsize is a function of Riskedamount and our stoploss.

12. We place our trade with all the input variables we have selected from the beginning in the function.

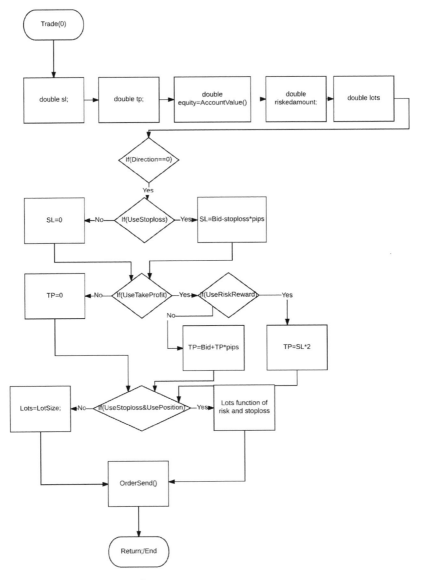

13-2 Flowchart of Trade() function.

We call on Trade(0) function which checks for If Direction is equal to zero, indicating the input function is equal to zero. If that is true it will run thru everything stated between the opening and closing brackets of if(Direction==0) statement and will run everything we have stated in the flowchart above.

```
10
11 extern int TakeProfit=50;
12 extern int StopLoss=25;
13 extern double LotSize=0.01;
14
15 double pips;
16
17 extern bool UseBreakEven=True;
18 extern int MoveToBreakEven=50;
19 extern int PipsProfitLock=20;
20
21 extern bool UseTrailingStop=true;
22 extern int WhenToTrail=50;
23 extern int TrailAmount=30;
24 extern bool UseStoploss=true;
25 extern bool UseTakeProfit=true;
26 extern bool UsePosition=true;
27 extern bool UseRiskReward=true;
28 extern double reward_ratio=2;
29 extern int RiskPercent=1;
30
31
```

13-3 Above you see how our global area looks.

How to use Trade()

We will use this function later, when we make a function Strategy() where we write trade logic and from that call on this Trade() function.

CandleClose Function

Function description

There are different ways to close a trade, some traders close with a stop loss and take profit, others use close after some candle rule. We create this function because we also need it to create a strategy.

Function name: CandleClose();

Variables in Global area:

extern Bool UseCandleClose=true; This variable is placed in the global area and is an extern variable because we need it to be changeable. If we want to use CandleClose() we set it to true or false.

extern int CloseAfterCandles=1; This is an integer variable and will decide after how many candles do we want to close our order. 1 means we want to close this trade after one candle trade has been executed.

Where to apply the function: The function should run on every tick if one order is open. It is placed within the same bracket as our BreakEven and TrailingStop function.

Variables in Local area:

Int period=Period(); This variable is assigned function Period(), period returns the value of which time period we are running this algo on. If we are running one minute chart it will return 1, and 5 if we are running five minute, 60 if are running on hourly and 240 if we are running on 4 hour which is 1 hour*4=60*4=240.

int period2=0; This variable has initially a value of zero because by using a switch function we want to assign a value to it. This variable will return timeframe seconds. For example if it's attached to one minute, there are 60 seconds in one minute, so then period2 has value of 60. If it is attached to 1 hour chart there are 60*60=3600 seconds in one hour so this variable will get a value of 3600, but this is done by using a switch function.

```
void CandleClose()//1
{
    int period=Period();//2.
    int period2=0;//3.

    switch(period)//4.
    {   case 1:period2=60;break;
        case 5:period2=300;break;
        case 15:period2=900;break;
        case 30:period2=1800;break;
        case 60:period2=3600;break;
        case 240:period2=14400;break;
        case 1440:period2=86400;break;
        case 10080:period2=604800;break;
        case 43200:period2=2592000;break;
        //default: Alert("Nothing");
    }

for(int i=OrdersTotal();i>0;i--)//5.
    {
    if(OrderSelect(i-1,SELECT_BY_POS,MODE_TRADES))//6.
        {
        if(TimeCurrent()-
OrderOpenTime()>period2*CloseAfterCandles)//7.
            {
            CloseAllOrders();//8.
            }
        }
    }
    return;
}
```

14-1 The CloseCandle() Function

1. We begin writing the type of function which is void. Then we name the function which is *CancleClose* and write opening and closing parentheses after the function name to alert the system that this is a function. Next we need an opening and a closing bracket which has all the operations within the function. Before the closing bracket we need to write *return;* to indicate

that this is the end of the function and control is be passed out of the function to the next operation, either it is executing the next function or ending.

2. We have to define our variable period as an integer, and assign value Period() which will return the timeframe this algo is running on. If it's one minute timeframe it will return 1 and 60 if its hourly, and 240 if it's 4 hour timeframe.

3. This is our next variable in local area, variable which can only be used within this function. This variable is an integer, and initially we assign a value of 0, but it will be given a value after we have run the switch operation which is next in the function. The name of this function is *period2*.

4. This is a switch operator, it's the same as an if-statement but with more cases. You begin by writing switch with opening and closing parentheses, in the parentheses you write the name of the variable you want to check. Until now *period* would have been given a value return by the *period()* function. Then you add an open and closing brackets to state all the cases. We have a number if that *period* has been assigned value 1, we will assign a value of 60 to variable period2 because it is 60 seconds in one minute. If that's the case after assigning the value we have written *break;* what this operator does is instead of that after assigning value *period2* and case is *period 1* it will not check the rest of the cases and pass the control out of the switch operator brackets to the next operation in the function. This way we save some time, but if we don't write break; it will continue to check whether case is 5,15 and so on. We have assigned a value to all variables that we need in the future operations both variables *period* and *period2*

5. Then we have a for loop which will run thru all open orders, starting with the latest order and decrease one by one.

6. We need to select an order in our trade pool to check the trade in the next operation.

7. Here we have an if-statement meaning decision statement. Function TimeCurrent() returns second current seconds since 1970, the number of seconds since 1970. OrderOpenTime() returns how many seconds have passed since 1970 when we execute the trade. The difference between these two is how many seconds the trade has been open. Period2 has the value we have assigned it using the switch operator. If we are running this strategy on a hourly chart, *period2* has a value of 3600(number of seconds in one hour) and we multiply this by the number of candles or hours after we want to close. 1 if we want to close after one hour and 2 etc if want to close this trade after two hourly candles(two hours). This if statement checks when the trade duration time in seconds is more than value on the right side of > if that's the case then it passes the control to the next operation.

8. Next operation is calling on our function CloseAllOrder(); which we already have built and is in the same script. It closes all open orders and delete pending orders.

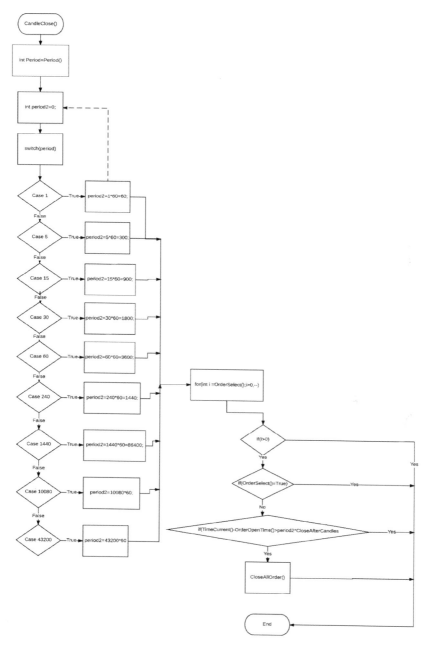

14-2 Flowchart of the CloseCandle() function.

```
11 extern int TakeProfit=50;
12 extern int StopLoss=25;
13 extern double LotSize=0.01;
14
15 double pips;
16
17 extern bool UseBreakEven=True;
18 extern int MoveToBreakEven=50;
19 extern int PipsProfitLock=20;
20
21 extern bool UseTrailingStop=true;
22 extern int WhenToTrail=50;
23 extern int TrailAmount=30;
24 extern bool UseStoploss=true;
25 extern bool UseTakeProfit=true;
26 extern bool UsePosition=true;
27 extern bool UseRiskReward=true;
28 extern double reward_ratio=2;
29 extern int RiskPercent=1;
30 extern bool UseCandleClose=true;
31 extern int CloseAfterCandles=1;
```

14-3 This is the global variable with CandleClose() function.

How to use CandleClose function

Now we have built a function which we will use to design our trading strategy. We must set UseCandleClose=true; and decide the candle number we want to close after in the global area. When we are using this function you must set UseStopLoss and UseTakeProfit as false otherwise you will get two closing mechanisms.

```
void OnTick()
  {
  if(IsNewCandle())
     {
      if(TotalOpenOrders()<1)
         {
         EntrySignal();
         }
     }
     if(TotalOpenOrders()>0)
        {
        if(UseBreakEven)
           {
           BreakEven();
           }
        if(UseTrailingStop)
           {
           TrailingStop();
           }
         if(UseCandleClose)
           {
           CandleClose();
           }
        }
  }
```

14-4 This is the OnTick() function with the candle close function included.

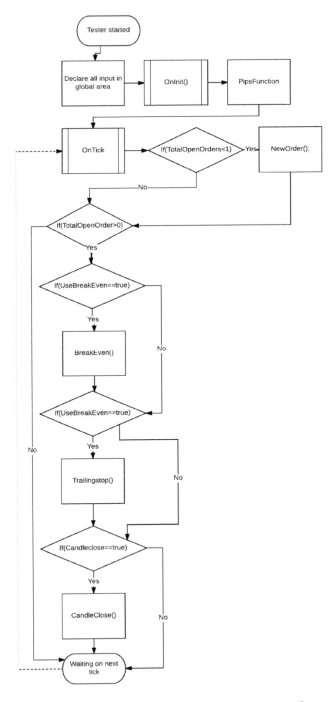

14-5 The flowchart for Ontick() function with Candleclose().

Strategy Function

Function description

This is the function where we decide on our strategy. We call on function Trade(0) for a buy order and Trade(1) for a sell order.

Function name: EntrySignal()

Variables in the Global Area:

Extern int ShortMAPeriod=50; This is the input to the moving average function of Shorter term and how many periods we are using of shorter term.

Extern int LongMAPeriod=100; This is the input to the moving average function of longer term, as moving average periods.

extern bool TradeLong=true; This variable is true if we want to trade long in our strategy.

extern bool TradeShort=true; This variable is true if we want to trade short in our strategy.

Variables in Functions Local Area:

We need to calculate the different moving averages. Because we are going to trade on crossovers we need to calculate one period and two periods prior moving averages. For the long trade the two periods prior short term moving average should be below the long term moving average and the one period prior, the short term should be above the long term and then we have a crossover strategy.

Double
ShortMaCurrent=iMA(Symbol(),PERIOD_CURRENT,ShortMAPeriod,0,MODE_SMA,PRICE_CLOSE,1);

Double
LongMaCurrent=iMA(Symbol(),PERIOD_CURRENT,LongMAPeri
od,0,MODE_SMA,PRICE_CLOSE,1);

Double
ShortMaPrevious=iMA(Symbol(),PERIOD_CURRENT,ShortMAPer
iod,0,MODE_SMA,PRICE_CLOSE,2);

Double
LongMaPrevious=iMA(Symbol(),PERIOD_CURRENT,LongMAPeri
od,0,MODE_SMA,PRICE_CLOSE,2);

You see that global variables which are changeable are the input in the local variables.

```
void EntrySignal()//0
{
double
ShortMaCurrent=iMA(Symbol(),PERIOD_CURRENT,ShortMAPeriod,0,MODE_SMA,PRICE_C
LOSE,1);//1.
double
LongMaCurrent=iMA(Symbol(),PERIOD_CURRENT,LongMAPeriod,0,MODE_SMA,PRICE_CLO
SE,1);
double
ShortMaPrevious=iMA(Symbol(),PERIOD_CURRENT,ShortMAPeriod,0,MODE_SMA,PRICE_
CLOSE,2);
double
LongMaPrevious=iMA(Symbol(),PERIOD_CURRENT,LongMAPeriod,0,MODE_SMA,PRICE_CL
OSE,2);

    if(TradeLong)//.2
    {
        if(ShortMaPrevious<LongMaPrevious &&
ShortMaCurrent>LongMaCurrent)//3.
        {
        Trade(0);//.4
        }
    }
    if(TradeShort)
    {
        if(ShortMaPrevious>LongMaPrevious && ShortMaCurrent<LongMaCurrent)
        {
        Trade(1);
        }
    }
return;
}
```

15-1 This how our strategy function will appear with the moving average crossover.

0. We begin by writing void because this function only executes

what is stated within its brackets, then the function name with open and closing parentheses. We then add an opening and closing bracket with *return;* in it.

1. We write the local variables we will use in this function and see that local variables have global extern variables as input variables.

2. We check if we have set our TradeLong bool variable to true or false, if it's true it passes control to the next operation.

3. This is also an if-statement which checks if the two period short moving average was below the slow moving average and one period fast moving average is above one period slow moving average meaning checks for a cross. If the cross has happened then it will call on the function Trade() with 0 input variable which means buy orders.

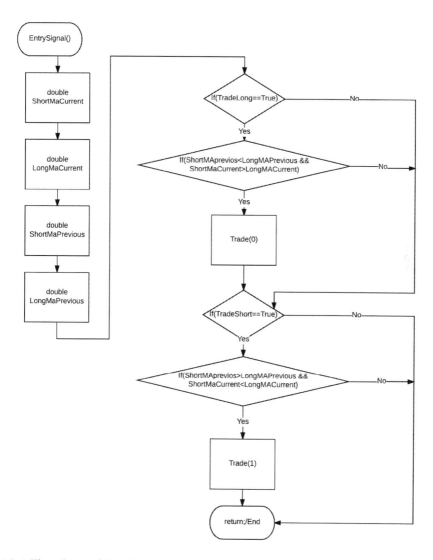

15-2 Flowchart of the Entry Signal

```
 1 //+----------------------------------------------------------------+
 2 //|                                                      MyAlgo.mq4 |
 3 //|                                                    Tayyab Rashid |
 4 //|                                             www.tayyabrashid.com |
 5 //+----------------------------------------------------------------+
 6 #property copyright "Tayyab Rashid"
 7 #property link       "www.tayyabrashid.com"
 8 #property version    "1.00"
 9 #property strict
10
11 extern int TakeProfit=50;
12 extern int StopLoss=25;
13 extern double LotSize=0.01;
14
15 double pips;
16
17 extern bool UseBreakEven=True;
18 extern int MoveToBreakEven=50;
19 extern int PipsProfitLock=20;
20
21 extern bool UseTrailingStop=true;
22 extern int WhenToTrail=50;
23 extern int TrailAmount=30;
24 extern bool UseStoploss=true;
25 extern bool UseTakeProfit=true;
26 extern bool UsePosition=true;
27 extern bool UseRiskReward=true;
28 extern double reward_ratio=2;
29 extern int RiskPercent=1;
30 extern bool UseCandleClose=true;
31 extern int CloseAfterCandles=1;
32 extern bool TradeLong=true;
33 extern bool TradeShort=true;
34 extern int ShortMAPeriod=50;
35 extern int LongMAPeriod=100;
36
```

15-3 This is the variable in the global area with all the functions included also EntrySignal().

124

How to use the OnTick() function

We will place the EntrySignal() in our Ontick function and within the brackets of IsNewCandle() and TotalOpenOrders<1 if-statement.

```
void OnTick()
  {
  if(IsNewCandle())
    {
     if(TotalOpenOrders()<1)
       {
         EntrySignal();
       }
    }
    if(TotalOpenOrders()>0)
       {
       if(UseBreakEven)
          {
          BreakEven();
          }
       if(UseTrailingStop)
          {
          TrailingStop();
          }
        if(UseCandleClose)
          {
          CandleClose();
          }
       }
  }
```

16-1 This is the OnTick() function with EntrySignal() function included.

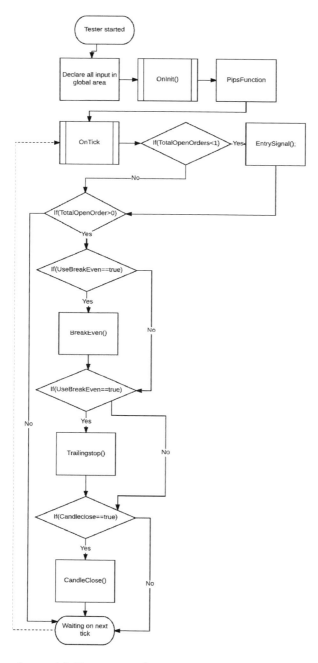

16-2 Flowchart with EntrySignal() function included.

Designing a Trading Strategy

First, ask yourself why do you want to trade. As long as you are in the market your capital is at risk. You can take big risks to make big rewards which equals gambling techniques, or you can trade wisely and control your risk to make reasonable profits in the long term. Professional traders make yearly approx. 7%, on average, a drawdown which is acceptable is double of your return.

You now have the building blocks that you can use along with the freedom to adjust them and they will still remain effective. To avoid curve fitting, you need a system that includes volatility parameters but you must not over optimize or optimize several different parameters at once.

Trading strategy development

1. Find an entry signal, this is accomplished by changing the EntrySignal() function and put your own trading logic and set CandleClose()(Stoploss, Takeprofit, Breakeven and Trailing function to false because we will not use any of them). Close the position after 5-10-20-30 candles and see which type of entry signal it is, it should generate a positive overall return. Then it's worth going further with this trading signal.

2. Remember to have a significant test time period, plus include many types of markets, uptrend, downtrend and ranging markets. Volatile uptrend, average volatility uptrend and excess volatility, are also included in your test. Run the same entry logic on different pairs and different timeframes to find out which one is best. You will quickly understand that a breakout entry will have a positive overall return when you use candle close and choose to close just after 5-10 candles, but a trend strategy will need more time to be in profit. So based on your trading strategy you should be able to narrow your close after a number of candles parameter. Often there is not

the same open and closing mechanism for long and short trades, so you might first find a strategy for long and then one for short.

3. When you have chosen the timeframe and a good performing pair. You try to combine your entry strategy with different exit strategies. It could be a dynamic stop-loss and take-profit, trailing stop, 60 period simple moving average trailing stop, with or without breakeven. You should have predefined rules.

4. To be successful you need a diversified portfolio of strategies on different pairs and timeframes. Because if you have a trend strategy it will lose money in ranging market but if you also have a strategy for ranging markets you will make money on that.

5. Whatever system you have, return to drawdown ratio can be as large as 1:2.

6. Sometimes it might be best to go the other way around and design an exit system(what you want from the market), and then design a entry signal.

If-Statement

This is frequently used in functions and it is decision making, or in other words we ask the question whether a statement is true or not.

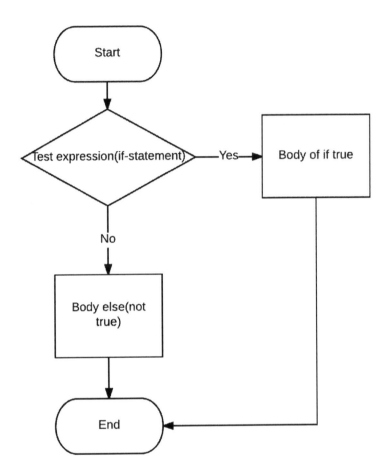

This is a flow chart of an if-statement.

From start, pass the control to if-statement. If the statement is true then everything in the *Body of true* is executed. But if that's not the case and the statement is not true but false, then everything in body else will be executed, and both will pass control to the *end.*

Code: Binary Extra, Redeem at www.gcmsonline.info at contact us.

Example 1:

```
void Test1()
{
    int A=2;
    int B=3;
    if(A>B)
    {
        Comment("A is bigger Than B");
    }
    else
    {
        Comment("A is less than B");
    }
return;
}
```

This is an example of an if-statement, we have a function called Test1. It starts with defining two variables A and B.

Then we have an if-statement which ask whether A is bigger than B. Then if that's true we have an output comment which is "A is bigger than B". If the statement is false, A is less than B, then we have else body which will be executed. A comment "A is less than B".

Example 2:

```
void Test2()
{
    int A=2;
    int B=3;
    if(A>B)
    {
        Comment("A is bigger Than B");
    }
return;
}
```

This is another type of using if-statement, it checks whether the statement is true, if it is true it will comment "A is bigger Than B" if it is not true it will just pass the control to the end. You can see the flowchart of it below.

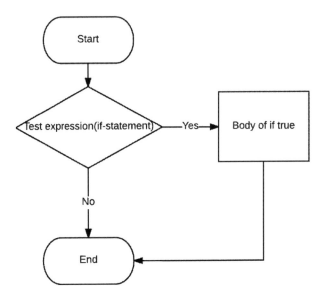

If-statement without else statements.

For Loop Function

You can use for or while loop. We use a for loop.

Example of for loop:

```
void test2()
{
    int Number=0;
    for(int i=3;i>0;i--)
    {
        Number=Number+1;
    }
}
```

Example on a for loop

Here we have a function called test2, which begins by declaring a variable Number as integer and assigning value of zero. Then we run a for loop.

We start by writing for and two parentheses as a function with an opening and closing bracket. In the parentheses, we write three variables. First variable is how many times we want to run this function or loop which we will define between the opening and closing bracket, it will execute everything between them each loop. The second variable is how long do we want to loop, as long as i is more than zero. The third variable defined which is either style ascending or descending. ++ means it will start with number one and then loop 2 and 3. - - means it will start with 3 then loop 2 and 1, and stop there because we want to loop as long as i is above 0. In the opening and closing brackets we write everything we want to execute on each loop.

Below is the flowchart of the loop above.

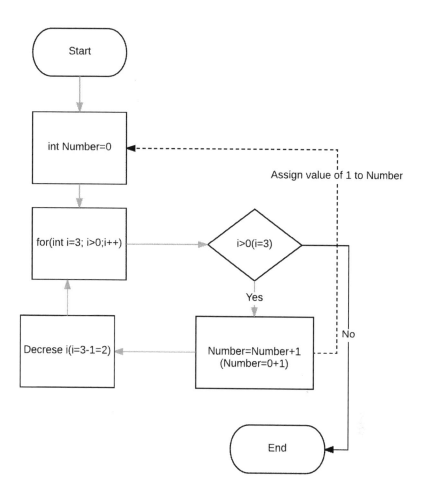

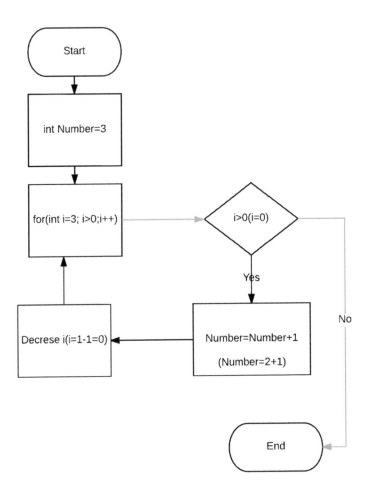

Advanced Forex Strategies

Introduction

This section will expand your trading knowledge even more as we dive deep into advanced strategies for forex.

As an investor or trader you will at some point come across online posts which state "best break out strategy." You will also find research articles and books explaining the average returns of various strategies and providing statistics on them. Now what if you ask yourself, "do they work?" and you then begin the testing process. As a trader it's important to know how the simulated results are calculated and you will also need them be as precise as possible. Let us proceed to test some different strategies and trading systems.

NOTE: The format of the first three chapters is in the form of a trade adventure where a strategy will be introduced, tested, and then finally refined.

The Day Of The Week Anomaly

Daily High - Low

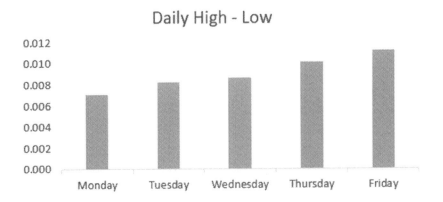

Research has shown that stocks and other markets tend to move more on Fridays than Mondays. To test this my colleague and I gathered back-data from 2001 - 20016. We used an approximately 80/20 split where 80% was in sample and the remainder out of sample.

Note: In Sample - Out of Sample: It is statistics speak which in most cases means using past data to make forecasts of the future. In sample refers to the data that you have and out of sample to the data you don't have but want to forecast or estimate.

The Signal

Forex was the main market for our test. To begin we had the issue with Daylight Savings Time which required that we offset the time settings. Then we needed to select which time of the day would be optimal for the trade, should we use the European, New York or the Asian session close. To keep things relatively simple we just bought on the open of the day Friday (European), and held the positions to the open of the next day.

The Day of The Week Effect for Friday, we bought at 00.00 and sold 00.00 on Monday. This required that we had to take into account the gap (weekend), but we did not consider it a big issue. Time was also not a significant factor because the real volatility triggers are when the market is open. Therefore, if we did not close Friday evening but held the positions open until Monday it would have not had a noticeable impact because the market does not move when it is closed.

Data

Our in sample time period was 01.01.2001 - 31.12.2011 and out of sample time period was 01.01.2012 - 01.06.2016. The instrument traded was EURUSD.

Basic Strategy

We began with the basic strategy and without any changes of parameters. The strategy is buy on the first tick after 00.00 Friday and sell on the first price move on Monday (00.00). This is something different from what has been provided by previous studies using excel or any other program measuring the average price change from the day of open to close (next day open). We used tick data and a simulator that simulated the real trading environment to get our results as precise as possible.

Note: Tick: A tick is a measure of the minimum upward or downward movement in the price of a security. A tick can also refer to the change in the price of a security from trade to trade.

First Results

To begin we did not include any stop-loss or take-profit. We also did not make any other adjustments on the strategy, our testing period was 01.01.2005 - 26.08.2016.

The results were the following:

Results	
Average profi	-1.57
Sum profit	-897.84
Winning trade	297
Total trades	572
Standard dev	96.55
Relnumber	-0.39

They were disappointing, the total loss was -897 USD. Clearly, the basic strategy was in need of some fine-tuning to improve our results.

Adding Trend Filter Exponential Moving Average

We applied the trend filter 20 EMA, 60 EMA, and 100 EMA. An Exponential Moving Average (EMA) is a type of moving average that is similar to a Simple Moving Average, except that more weight is given to the latest data. It is also known as the Exponentially Weighted Moving Average. This type of moving average reacts faster to recent price changes than a Simple Moving Average. For some this may appear random but this filter was chosen because of the number of days it counts.

20 EMA = 20 trading days in a month
60 EMA = 60 trading days equals three months
100 EMA = 100 trading days equals five months

Trend filter: 20EMA>60EMA>100EMA

The chart illustrates the trend filter:

You can see that it only opened trades when the 20 EMA (top line) is above 60 EMA (in middle) and 60 EMA is above 100 EMA (bottom). I could have only used 20 EMA>100 EMA but that would have had more volatility or false entry signals. I wanted both the long term (60 EMA>100 EMA) and short term (20 EMA>60 EMA) trends to be up.

We got the following results:

	Average profit	Sum profit	Winning trade	Total trades	Standard dev	Relnumber
The Basic Strategy	-2	-898	297	572	97	-0.39
20EMA>60EMA>100EMA	6	1832	178	322	86	1.19
20EMA<60EMA<100EMA	-12	-1831	68	147	103	-1.47

To compare two or more systems it is not enough to only examine the profits. This is because profit is only one of the indicators. What is equally important is the number of trades and volatility. It does not make sense to have one system with just one big or a few profitable trades and many losses. Those few profitable trades could be random, they could be Black Swans which most likely will not repeat in the future, therefore we did not want too much variance. The formula for the Rel number that we will refer to is:

$$Rel = \frac{\text{Average profit}}{\text{Standard deviation of profit}} * \sqrt{\# \; of \; trades}$$

You can typically expect better returns from a strategy with many trades than one with only a few. To summarize, the higher the Rel number the better the trading system.

One thing we can conclude is that by applying the filter for an uptrend we had better returns than the basic strategy. The other is that this strategy works better in an uptrend market than in a downtrend, we had negative returns in a down market. We also had a better Rel number with a trend filter.

Volatility Filter

Our opinion is that volatility is also an important indicator. Volatility is constantly changing so comparing recent volatility will also make sense. We compared the 10 days average range to the 1 day average range. This allowed us to see excess volatility and the opposite. Using these settings is the same as saying today's volatility compared to the average volatility of last 10 trading days (two weeks).

We saw the following results:

	Average profit	Sum profit	Winning trade	Total trades	Standard dev	Relnumber
The Basic Strategy	-2	-898	297	572	97	-0.39
20EMA>60EMA>100EMA	6	1832	178	322	86	1.19
20EMA<60EMA<100EMA	-12	-1831	68	147	103	-1.47
ATR(1)>ATR(10)	-2	-356.74	73	143	82	-0.4
ATR(1)<ATR(10)	12	2188.62	105	179	88	1.9

The results showed that **excess volatility** on Thursdays destroyed this strategy, meaning if the range on the Thursday before is above the last two weeks volatility it's bad for the strategy. However, if the opposite is true, the range is less than the last ten days average range we will make money with this strategy. If you don't get it right away it will become clearer. For now just know it's clear that this strategy works well when there is an **uptrend** and **volatility is less** than the previous two weeks. As an investor or trader you will buy when you see that EURUSD is in an uptrend both short and long term. We also saw that we improved the Rel number, we made fewer trades but increased profits. A decrease in volatility increased our Rel number, which was good. Remember we did not want to gamble, we only traded when it was appropriate. Our Rel number has improved from 1.19 to 1.9.

Gambling or Investing With Calculated Risk = Stop-loss!

I typically avoid trading without a stop-loss, I need to know what I'm risking on each particular trade. Using my personal formula I figured that the right stop-loss for this strategy was 50 pips.

The results, introducing a stop-loss decreased the volatility. You can see (Table 1) that we improved the Rel number and decreased the number of winning trades. The increase in Rel number meant that there were several trades which moved more than 50 pips against us before they went into profit again. This for me is similar to gambling, I would rather exclude such trades and set a stop-loss at 50 pips.

Position Sizing and Fixed % Per Trade

Have you ever executed a trade without considering that if you lose above a fixed percent of your equity then you should close the trade? In trading this is not recommended, I never open a trade without calculating the risk. We will now move onto the concept of a fixed percent trade. This is where the lot size will be a function of our stop-loss and a risk tolerance of 1%. You take more risk when your equity increases and take less when your equity decreases.

With position sizing we increased our overall profit, but we also increased the volatility in our equity curve, so our Rel number decreased slightly. I would rather include position sizing than to rely on a higher Rel number.

Table 1

	Average profit	Sum profit	Winning trade	Total trades	Standard dev	Relnumber
The Basic Strategy	-2	-898	297	572	97	-0.39
20EMA>60EMA>100EMA	6	1832	178	322	86	1.19
20EMA<60EMA<100EMA	-12	-1831	68	147	103	-1.47
ATR(1)>ATR(10)	-2	-356.74	73	143	82	-0.4
ATR(1)<ATR(10)	12	2188.62	105	179	88	1.9
50 pips SL	11	2024.08	87	179	66	2.3
Position sizing	13	2280	85	179	77	2.22

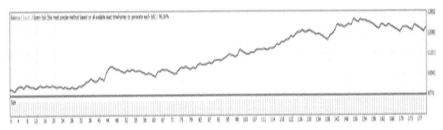

Equity curve in sample with position sizing

Out of Sample Test

We did an out of sample test in the period 01.01.2012 - 01.08.2016

	Average profit	Sum profit	Winning trade	Total trades	Standard dev	Relnumber
The Basic Strategy	-2	-898	297	572	97	-0.39
20EMA>60EMA>100EMA	6	1832	178	322	86	1.19
20EMA<60EMA<100EMA	-12	-1831	68	147	103	-1.47
ATR(1)>ATR(10)	-2	-356.74	73	143	82	-0.4
ATR(1)<ATR(10)	12	2188.62	105	179	88	1.9
50 pips SL	11	2024.08	87	179	66	2.3
Position sizing	13	2280	85	179	77	2.22
Out of sample	5	189	19	37	49	1

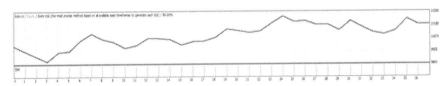

Equity curve out of sample

The results were not that promising we had a sum profit of 189 USD, the start equity was 10,000 USD so this equals a 1.89 % return. We also got a smaller Rel number which was not that good. The maximum drawdown received of 289 USD was way above the sum profit. Obviously, I was unsatisfied with these results.

Summary

We have taken several steps to improve the Day of The Week strategy. What we can say for sure is that you will not make any money when you include transaction costs in the basic strategy. This strategy works best in an uptrend market. As an experienced trader I believed that the timeframe might be the problem. The strategy could have been more profitable but we were not giving it enough time. The stop-loss of 50 pips is enough, but on the other side we closed our trade on Monday whatever the results were. Further refinement is needed.

We will keep the same entry strategy for the next chapter but the trade management needs to be different. When making trades with this it will be necessary to include a take profit function of the weekly volatility or trailing stop. These needed improvements will be seen in the next chapters.

First Refinement: Day of The Week Effect Strategy

We move forward to make our first adjustment to the Day of The Week Effect strategy from the last chapter. What I will point to as the weakness with the Day of The Week Effect is the traditional way to trade it. This weakness is to close the trade on Monday morning because you are taking some risk even when you are using a stop-loss. However, if we are not giving the trade enough time then we will not get the maximum possible profit. A simple but respected rule of trading is to "cut your losses and let your profits run."

After examining the strategy, I realized that it only made money because it had some good trades that moved 300-400 pips during one day. Unfortunately, this is infrequent and includes many drawdowns that I would prefer not to have in my portfolio. We will now see the difference in equity using some different ways to manage the trade, our entry signal remains the same. You will also see why it is important to include volatility in the planning.

Method

Using the same trading signal, but on Friday we opened with 20EMA>60EMA (we have excluded the 100 EMA this time). Lot size is 0.1 and an account starting balance of 10,000 USD. The closing statement of Monday was removed and we just had a stop-loss and take-profit. We split the data, in sample and out of sample. In sample we optimized the different parameters and then performed an out of sample test to see whether or not the optimized strategy works well. We also increased the range of our in sample data to 01.01.1990 -01.01.2012. We used a tight stop-loss, trailing stop and break-even, we called this method *No Vols* because we did not include volatility in any of the tests.

Stop-Loss and Take-Profit

Our strategy optimized the stop-loss and take-profit between 100 - 600 to see whether the results hold. It delivered an optimal stop-loss of 400 and take profit of 600. We received total profits of 86,413 USD and Rel number of 7.09 which we could not yet compare because in this test we had included an additional 11 years of prior data. It was necessary to combine this with other trade management methods and see which one was the best to manage after a trade had been executed. What we could compare was the average profit, it had increased to 138 USD, where it wasn't more than 2,2 in the earlier test, just because we allowed our trade to run longer.

Method	Average profit	Sum profit	Total # of trades	Winning # of Trades	Standard deviation of profit	Rel #
Only SL & TP	138 $	86,413	357	626	486.8007082	7.09

Graph showing equity with stop-loss and take-profit
Here and on our other graphs SL=Stop-Loss and TP=Take-profit

Stop-loss, Take-profit and Break-even

Most traders are familiar with break-even, this is where you amend your stops when the market has moved a certain amount in your favor and this was included in our strategy. Break-even is good to have because if you don't use one, there is a risk that even after having a profit you end the trade with a loss. We saw 71,480 USD in profits and 6.99 of Rel number, a bit smaller than without use of a break-even. It decreased the volatility in the equity curve, but also decreased the profit, meaning sometimes we were stopped out because we had changed our stop-loss to break-even, so this was a trade-off between risk-reward, we decreased our risk, but we also got lower returns.

Method	Average profit		Sum profit	Total # of trades	Winning # of Trades	Standard deviation of profit	Rel #
Only SL & TP	138	$	86,413	357	626	487	7.09
SL & TP & Breakeven	114	$	71,480	428	626	408	6.99

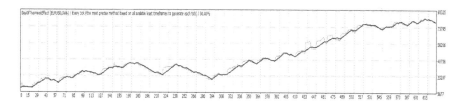

Graph showing equity with the break-even function, we got a smoother equity curve

Stop-loss and Trailing stop

In this strategy we used Moving Averages, we placed trades when the market was in an uptrend. It is important for you to remember the trader saying, "cut your losses and let your profit run." It's correct to have a stop-loss, but a predefined take profit would limit our profits in an uptrend because we don't know exactly how high it will go. Therefore, we had to exclude the take-profit and instead added a trailing stop function. We increased our average profit to 350 USD per trade, increased our overall profits to 213,636 USD and our Rel number to 9.89. When we included the break-even function we only had 151,194 USD for a profit and a 8.20 Rel number which was lower than what we received with using only a stop-loss and trailing stop. I will not include the break-even function in the future for this strategy. We will trail the stop below recent higher lows.

Method	Average profit		Sum profit	Total # of trades	Winning # of Trades	Standard deviation of profit	Rel #
Only SL & TP	138	$	86,413	357	626	487	7.09
SL & TP & Breakeven	114	$	71,480	428	626	408	6.99
SL & TP & Trailingstop	350	$	213,636	305	610	875	9.89
SL & TP & Breakeven & Trailingstop	242	$	151,194	425	626	737	8.20

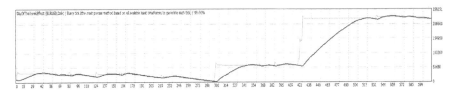

Graph showing equity with stop-loss and trailing stop functions

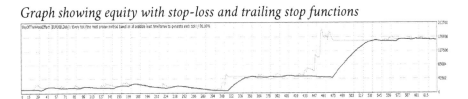

Graph showing equity with stop-loss, break-even and trailing stop functions

Out of Sample Test

The out of sample test period was 01.01.2012 - 01.09.2016. We experienced disappointing results, to be more direct, we lost all of our trading capital and got stopped out. As traders we want to know if our results will be valid in the future. We also know that there are different ways to manage trades that will improve our results.

Volatility is very important, EURUSD had been trading in a range since 2014, therefore you should not use a stop-loss and take-profit optimized in the period before it, none of the trade management tools are dynamic or valid without taking an account of the volatility.

Method	Average profit	Sum profit	Total # of trades	Winning # of Trades	Standard deviation of profit	Rel #
Only SL & TP	138 $	86,413	357	626	487	7.09
SL & TP & Breakeven	114 $	71,480	428	626	408	6.99
SL & TP & Trailingstop	350 $	213,636	305	610	875	9.89
SL & TP & Breakeven & Trailingstop	242 $	151,194	425	626	737	8.20
Out of Sample	-127 $	(9,770)	22	77	216	-5.16

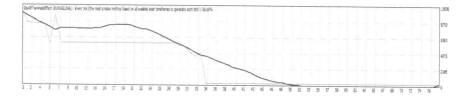

Graph showing equity out of sample test results

Summary

We showed the importance of different trade management styles and the importance of volatility in our strategy. The current market could be different from the market we had during our testing period. EURUSD was our test pair and in the background, 2013, the American and European stock markets were at all-time highs, people were waiting for a crash or an excuse for the pair to get out of the continuation pattern to either the up or downside.
It had been trading within a very tight range.

It is important to keep in mind that your strategy will fail if you don't account for the volatility in the market. If you are day trading and use a stop-loss of 20 pips and a take profit of 100 pips but you see that on average the daily range has been 60 pips, you will never hit your take profit. If you have a trend strategy you will never achieve the full potential of the trade if you just use take-profit, it's much better to trail the stop below the recent high or low. You can see from the equity curve graph where we only had a stop-loss and trailing stop in the first half of the trade we did not gain much profits. This was because at that time the range was not as wide. Therefore using just take profit and stop-loss would not have delivered optimal results. One alternative is to re-optimize the parameters each month using the previous year or quarterly data and I prefer to use volatility based parameters.

Day of The Week Effect: Introducing Volatility

In the previous chapters we have focused on the Day of The Week Effect anomaly and how it could be improved. We will continue to enhance the strategy by introducing volatility.

Any trader will tell you that volatility is dynamic, it is constantly changing, sometimes we have excess volatility other times we have a contraction. If you optimize your strategy when the market has excess volatility and then at trade execution time there is a decrease in volatility you most likely will not hit your take-profit level. What you will instead experience is that your stops are frequently hit. It is important that your risk and reward levels are a function of current market volatility. Right before Brexit, for example, GBPUSD moved a lot more than its normal price movement pattern. We saw excess volatility because there were numerous conflicting and often confusing news reports before the last vote. If you as a day trader had placed a trade with a 20 pips stop-loss, you would have often experienced that your trades would hit the stop-loss and then quickly reversed after hitting it. We showed earlier how poor the results could be when we did not calculate for the volatility. Now I will show the difference of when you include volatility in your trade management.

Method

Keeping our Day of The Week Effect strategy, we opened the trade on the first tick on Friday. The pair tested was the same as used in the previous examples, EURUSD. Our in sample test period was 01.01.1990 - 01.01.2012. The starting balance was 10,000 USD and the amount per trade was 0.1 lot. We implemented one change in our entry signal compared to our last trial. Earlier we mentioned that this is a trend strategy, in other words, we buy if the trend is up. This applies to both long and short-term trends. As traders we know that this can also give us many stop-loss executions if the market overshoots. If you just enter and buy at the market price it could be in a range and this normally gives a poor risk-reward ratio to the latest top. Therefore it is better to buy on pullbacks because then you have more of a distance to the previous top, and an improved risk-reward. The execution was the following: the long-term trend our 20 EMA was above the 60 EMA, however the shorter term trend the 5 EMA was below our 20 EMA. It's Friday, we opened the trade with our settings. We did not buy blindly, **but** on the pullbacks as experienced traders like to do. We had fewer trades but that was good.

Dynamic Stop-loss and Take-profit

We adjusted our stop-loss and take-profit as functions of the current volatility. This implies that it adjusted according to the current volatility and then we optimized the different parameters. We received the following results:

Method	Average profit	Sum Profit	# of winning trades	# of total trades	Standard deviation	Rel number
SL & TP	26.0	4497	98	173	234	1.46

Graph showing the equity curve using volatility stop-loss and take-profit

We got total profits of 4,497 USD during the test period and Rel number for 1.46 and average profit of 26 USD.

Dynamic Stop-Loss, Take-Profit and Break-Even

We then introduced a break-even which was a function of the current volatility and with this we increased the average profit to 33.9 USD, sum profit to 5,687 USD and Rel number to 2.05. There was decreased volatility in the equity curve, and also some of our losing trades became winning trades by adding a break-even. Using this function we also locked in some profits above our entry price.

Method	Average profit	Sum Profit	# of winning trades	# of total trades	Standard deviation	Rel number
SL & TP	26.0	4497	98	173	234	1.46
SL & TP & Breakeven	33.9	5867	108	173	218	2.05

Graph showing the equity curve using volatility stop-loss, take-profit and break-even, we got smoother equity curves

Trailing Stop

When using the trailing-stop below the previous lower high, we had some distance below the low of that candle. I also introduced this distance between the previous lower high and stop-loss as a function of recent volatility. In essence we didn't have a stop-loss, we allowed the trailing-stop to do the work, with this we saw the following results:

Method	Average profit	Sum Profit	# of winning trades	# of total trades	Standard deviation	Rel number
SL & TP	26.0	4497	98	173	234	1.46
SL & TP & Breakeven	33.9	5867	108	173	218	2.05
Trailing stop	87.4	15119	68	173	370	3.11
Trailing stop + Breakeven	95.8	16572	90	173	360	3.50

Graph showing the equity curve with only a trailing-stop

Graph showing the equity curve with trailing-stop and break-even

We saw that by using a trailing-stop we nearly tripled our average return, but we got less winning trades, the overall total profit increased to 15,119 USD also the Rel number increased to 3.11 which is an improvement. Then we introduced a break-even function where we locked in some profits after the market moved, this is also a function of volatility. We increased our profit and Rel number to 3.5, a noticeable difference. The last time we introduced break-even we got worse results than when we kept it out. This time when break-even was a function of volatility we got better results. However, what was more important were the out of sample results.

Out of Sample Test

We had been refining the strategy and the aim was to optimize it on in sample data and get good out of sample data. Our out of sample data was 01.01.2012 - 01.09.2016.

Method	Average profit	Sum Profit	# of winning trades	# of total trades	Standard deviation	Rel number
SL & TP	26.0	4497	98	173	234	1.46
SL & TP & Breakeven	33.9	5867	108	173	218	2.05
Trailing stop	87.4	15119	68	173	370	3.11
Trailing stop + Breakeven	95.8	16572	90	173	360	3.50
Out of sample test	37.3	1232	20	33	185	1.16

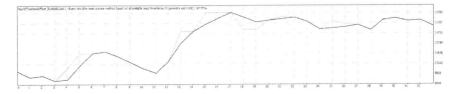

Graph showing the out of sample test

We had a sum profit of 1,232 USD and Rel number for 1.16, and 20 of the 33 trades were profitable. Actually, I was satisfied with the results because the pair, even though it had a downtrend at the start of 2014, it ended up ranging towards the end of the year. This uptrend strategy remained on the same levels during a range bound period which was good. More often than not, in the instances where the market goes from one sentiment to another, people usually experience huge losses. We however remained mostly level with only small drawdowns.

Summary

There is not much more to change or adjust on this method. It is time for us to decide whether or not the Day of The Week Effect strategy can be used. My conclusion is that it can be used and is still valid but not with the old way that traders have used it to manage trades. You should use break-evens and lock in some profits when a trade has moved your way. We saw that when we did not account for volatility, we got much better in sample results. We then lost all of our money in the out of sample period, when not accounting for the volatility. However, when we optimized accounting for the volatility we got acceptable out of sample results.

I would not recommend to anyone putting all their money on one pair. It is essential that you diversify your risk amongst uncorrelated currency pairs and uncorrelated securities. Therefore if one pair is ranging, not making much money or taking a loss, the other will be in an uptrend. Your losses in the ranging currency pair will be offset by larger profits from the currency pair that is in a trend. We ran this strategy to buy on different days, Mondays, Tuesdays, etc., used the same settings for managing the trade, we also received the results that Fridays were the best days to buy in an up-trending market.

What Are Realistic Profits To Target In The Market?

When many people begin trading, myself included, we are often told that it is a good way to make money within a short period of time. I developed some strategies and they did well to begin with but they also included huge drawdowns. With these types of results it is easy for one to conclude there must have been something wrong with the strategy. At one point I had 20% percent returns a month, which meant that I was doubling my capital within six months. In some months I even had 30% returns.

As good as the returns were, the dramatic drawdowns were a sign that things were far from perfect. I then went off on a mission in an attempt to discover what were the limits and what were realistic returns. Where to begin? should I read forums? Not really, they are usually filled with unvetted people bragging of doubling of their accounts in one month etc. without providing you access to their trade data. Unfortunately, even the trade data can be falsified.

I wanted to find out how other professionals were doing, comparing my results against the results of the institutional traders. These are the people who are paid generous salaries and bonuses to make money by trading or investing for the big investment funds and banks.

To accomplish my research goals, there were useful tools like the Barclay Currency Traders Index and the Barclay Systematic Traders Index. They track the results of more than 400 long term audited systematic and manual currency traders.

Systematic Traders

Year	Return	Year	Return	Year	Return
1980	-	1993	8.19%	2006	2.10%
1981	-	1994	-3.18%	2007	8.72%
1982	-	1995	15.27%	2008	18.16%
1983	-	1996	11.58%	2009	-3.38%
1984	-	1997	12.76%	2010	7.82%
1985	-	1998	8.12%	2011	-3.83%
1986	-	1999	-3.71%	2012	-3.20%
1987	63.01%	2000	9.89%	2013	-1.10%
1988	12.22%	2001	2.99%	2014	10.32%
1989	1.18%	2002	12.09%	2015	-2.92%
1990	34.58%	2003	8.71%	2016	0.32%[†]
1991	13.37%	2004	0.54%		
1992	3.25%	2005	0.95%		

[†]Estimated YTD performance for 2016 calculated with reported data as of October 21 2016 12:08 US CST

At a Glance from Jan 1987

Compound Annual Return	7.56%
Sharpe Ratio	0.34
Worst Drawdown	22.07%
Correlation vs S&P 500	-0.04
Correlation vs US Bonds	0.11
Correlation vs World Bonds	-0.04

The compounded yearly profits since 1987 is 7,56%

The Currency Traders

At a Glance from Jan 1987

Compound Annual Return	6.54%
Sharpe Ratio	0.32
Worst Drawdown	15.26%
Correlation vs S&P 500	-0.02
Correlation vs US Bonds	0.13
Correlation vs World Bonds	-0.02

Year	%	Year	%	Year	%
1980	-	1993	-3.33%	2006	-0.12%
1981	-	1994	-5.96%	2007	2.59%
1982	-	1995	11.49%	2008	3.50%
1983	-	1996	6.69%	2009	0.91%
1984	-	1997	11.35%	2010	3.45%
1985	-	1998	5.71%	2011	2.25%
1986	-	1999	3.12%	2012	1.71%
1987	29.56%	2000	4.45%	2013	0.87%
1988	4.28%	2001	2.71%	2014	3.35%
1989	18.89%	2002	6.29%	2015	4.65%
1990	57.74%	2003	11.08%	2016	0.25%[†]
1991	10.94%	2004	2.36%		
1992	10.27%	2005	-1.21%		

[†]Estimated YTD performance for 2016 calculated with reported data as of October 21-2016 12:08 US CST

The currency traders have experienced 6,54% compounded yearly profits since 1987.

The best fund had profit/maximum drawdown of 1 but the average was 0.5 for all of the funds. This means that the "big boys" also experienced drawdowns which were twice the returns. With a long-term view they were in profit overall.

You can check the Barclay indices here:
http://www.barclayhedge.com/research/indices/cta/sub/sys.html

Short Term Fast Growth vs Long Term Slow Growth

We will examine two ways of operating in the market, short term with fast growth and long term with slow growth. The driver behind fast growth is the high leverage that traders have access to in the markets. This leverage allows you to trade with much more market exposure than the funds that you have available in an account. This also means that you can open yourself to additional risks, some may even say that you are gambling. The risk of a total loss of capital can be high. The increased risk is coupled the opportunity to have faster growth. The second approach is to develop strategies that gives you smaller profits while at the same time having lower risk.

The first approach (fast and high-risk) is considered by many to be gambling with your capital and it regularly has a high rate of failure. Success, when it does occur is largely due to random luck and usually does not last for a significant period of time. There is only a small percentage of people who attempt fast and high-risk that gain any financial rewards.

Some of the individuals who do achieve significant profits through their initial high-risk ventures, leverage their success to live from that capital by later trading lower risk methods. However, as stated, the risk of a total loss of capital is high and the probabilities of success are low. I suggest that you strive to build capital gradually with a low drawdown strategy to keep the losses small.

Forex trading is about making calculated trades while keeping capital preservation and risk management in mind. Your initial aim is surviving in the market. Survival is one of the most important things for a trader and the reason why capital preservation should be executed in an aggressive manner. Controlling risk should be a priority before aiming for profits. You need to consider more of how you will avoid losing money to the market than how much capital you want to take out. As I say in the classes that I teach "make failure survivable." With this base and understanding that you have we can move towards the next set of strategies.

The Big Boys vs Small Traders

In this chapter I will reveal more insights about the financial markets, especially the differences between the average small trader and the institutions.

Averaging The Price Doesn't Make Sense

When I first began working as a trader it was common to hear "averaging the price." Initially it sounded odd and didn't make much sense to me. Why should people buy more of a security if it is falling? Just try to think about it as a rational person, would you invest more money where you are already experiencing losses? No, and it doesn't make any sense either to the average investor. We were also told "cut your losses and let your profits run", and that is a very good trading strategy. Another of the early lessons was that we should have at least a 1:2 risk/reward ratio. It is in our nature as opportunists, we usually prefer to bet when the expectation of gain is more in our favor. This is especially true when we know that the money we are investing will at least double when we are right, and lose less if we are wrong. Even a fool with only one banana doesn't want to bet it if he knows it will not return at least two, we want double of the amount we are risking.

Nothing Is Free, You Even Have to Pay For Water

When you find a good recipe, and if followed step by step you should have a tasty cake or a delicious dish in front of you. You were told that if followed exactly you would get this result. In a similar manner what we traders/investors do is we believe that if we read books, or watch videos and simply follow those instructions we will get a solid plan which will help us become successful. However, what we are forgetting, which is sometimes stated in these sources, is that we pay to learn trading. The profits do not come without risk. You have to risk a certain amount of money to get money from the market. You will read about the traditional

1:2 risk to reward ratio. What they are offering you is a cost of the book to wealth ratio. It is unlikely that someone will give away their complete trading strategies on how to become a millionaire or billionaire in a 25 dollar book while teaching you to have a 1:2 risk/reward ratio. It is not the full story, the 1:2 ratio has its merits, but no one will do that trade with you, even the smiling fool will refuse your offer of 25 Dollars if he knows some get rich quick strategy that *actually* works. Another reason why NO claims of instant riches are made anywhere in this book.

In the markets it is you against the rest of the trading world, the chances of winning are best for the most prepared. When you earn money, someone on the other side is losing some, it is not like earning profits on fruits that you are harvesting. Remember that you are taking money out of someone's pocket and they will *not* allow that to happen easily. Even withdrawing your own funds from a bank has a fee now a days, and yes you even pay for water which is a free natural source.

Solution to the problem

Let us suppose you used 4 years of your spare time, weekends and nights to become a successful trader. You read every trading book that you could possibly think about. Read numerous online sources that should help you to become successful, but nothing helped. Then you begin to think about what could be wrong with your approach when it seems that others are getting it right. A crucial mistake in judgement was to trust blindly some of the literature written about investing. This was the experience of a trader friend of mine. He then started adding philosophy books to his reading list. Philosophers are critical thinkers, it helped him to become critical and think differently, which are great qualities to have as a trader.

As I remember, my friend did not even trust doctors. For many people, doctors are one of the professions that they trust the most. You would probably trust a doctor more than a banker. That impulse of trust should not be as straight forward as you would think. Health literature, like financial literature is also based on empirical studies and findings where you have a hypothesis that you try to reject or prove significant. You attempt to link a cause and result, if you do A then B will happen. Keep in mind these studies, in noticeable numbers, are exposed to a lot of randomness which the authors probably have tried to "sell" you or by fitting a theory to the results. This reminds me of the saying: "If you torture the data enough, it will confess to anything." Also in these studies there is a 5% chance that the results may be wrong or not significant. The lesson is to be more thorough and not accept information without a rational assessment prior to making your decision.

To reinforce my point, you should try to buy a stock (on a demo account) the next time a financial newspaper has information about increased earnings reported by a listed company. This will provide a practical understanding of what I am writing about. I have seen many times where stocks plunged after such "good" news. Who pays the bill? the average investor, who makes the money? the professionals of course, that is why I recommend this practice of thinking critically and learn from people who are trading. For example, Warren Buffet is known for making good investment decisions which you also could copy but you need to have the similar objectives that he has. He is a long term value investor.

The Unpleasant Truth

This truth relates to how professional hedge and pension funds trade their money. For those seeking or needing another perspective on this I suggest that you watch the movie *The Big Short*. If you do not have time for the full movie you can watch the trailers on any of the free online video platforms to get an idea of what it is about. In the film, the big investment funds sold and sold even more when their initial positions were experiencing losses. These market players were able to hold their positions because they borrowed money for the margin requirements. In the movie they detailed how these people made billions of dollars in the last financial crisis. They were initially short and when the market went higher they shorted even more at the higher price, by the way, they did not use a stop-loss.

More on stop-losses. Investors like a Warren Buffet do not operate in the world of stop-losses. They do not look to exit on the drop in price of a long position. Buffet and institutional traders are not using stop-losses and they can afford not to because they have deep pockets. Investment funds can remain in a losing trade for a long time because it is just a small part of their larger portfolio and they have available an almost unimaginable amount of capital for the margin requirements.

This is from an article that explains how Buffet bought even more on a sell off:

Warren Buffett showed that the sell off in Wells Fargo & Co.'s stock this year has just made him love the banking giant even more, as he boosted his stake in the company to 504.3 million shares, according to regulatory filings.

Wells Fargo's WFC, -0.23% stock dropped 1.3% on Tuesday, which suggests Buffett has lost about $327.8 million on his stake on the day.

Link to the article: http://www.marketwatch.com/story/warren-buffett-buys-more-wells-fargo-stock-on-a-dip-2016-03-29

The guru was able to have an open position running a loss of $327.8 million, instead of showing any signs of concern he went on to increase his stake. The average investor would have difficulty keeping a cool head with a losing position of a few thousand dollars (USD). Hopefully the difference is becoming clearer now. Allow me to explain further on how things are vastly different when an average investor trades and when the big institutions are trading.

Average Trader:

He will open a long position in a security with too much risk of his total portfolio. Our trader knows that if this security falls below a certain amount it will hurt his account and he will be stopped out. Also if he does not close the position, there will be insufficient capital for further trades. To avoid this scenario the stop-loss is executed and a loss is taken on the trade. Our investor finds a new security and he rinses and repeats the strategy.

The Big Boys:

They have a trade plan, they typically have just a small portion of their portfolio invested in a single security and have an exit strategy. They have also done a "what if" analysis of their trade before they opened it. If they are long and the security falls it's a potential jackpot for them. These institutions get to buy more at a lower price, then buy again, maybe even double of their initial position. If everything goes wrong and the broker gives a margin call, they just borrow money from their network or negotiate the margin requirements.

What are most (not all), smaller and inexperienced traders unable to do? first, is to borrow huge sums of money with ease, second, which make things worse, they usually do not have an exit strategy or a trade plan. Many just want to open a trade without even giving it much thought.

The Martingale Strategy Explained

Here I will highlight and explain a technique that has made amazing profits over the span of 5-6 years in our test. The results are revealed near the end of the chapter!

The strategy that we will examine is called Martingale. Basically, it requires that you increase your lot size and buy more (if long) when your initial position is in the red. You do need to have some distance between the orders in order to give your trade some room. By the way, this strategy is also used by gamblers, just to provide full disclosure and warning.

The Martingale technique has been an interest of mine for some time, but it was difficult to fully grasp it by manual trading alone. Therefore my colleague and I wrote a script and created an algorithm. We had an entry signal along with our take-profit. The entry turned out to be not that good. The timeframe used was 30 minutes and a lot size of 0.01, along with a starting balance of 10,000 USD.

After the initial short position trade was executed we placed 5 sell limit pending orders above our entry signal.

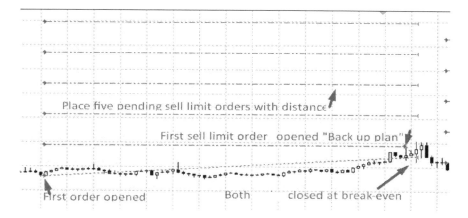

You can see on the graph that one of the pending orders was triggered, and quickly after, it closed both orders at break-even.

In another example of our strategy, we had two closing mechanisms. One is only used if the initial order opened, this is the strategy trigger, another one is used if one of the pending orders is triggered then we will close when we have a total open profit of 0, or break-even. If we were wrong we would have added to the losing position as back up. We did not optimize anything, the test pair was again EURUSD and the period was 01.01.2010 - 10.26.2010.

We saw the following results:

	Average profit	Sum profit	Winning trade	Total trades	Standard dev	Reinumber
0.1 Starting lot	45	20066	244	450	307	3
0.9 Starting lot	401	180598	244	450	2763	3
0.9 Starting lot and stoploss	207	86784	227	419	2710	1.6

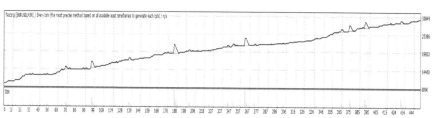

0.1 starting lot size

179

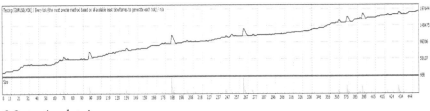

0.9 starting lot size

With stop-loss order instead of fifth pending order

We ran a back-test as low and high-risk. In the low-risk the initial trade had a lot size of 0.1 and with the high-risk test the initial lot size was higher at 0.9. With 0.1 we had around a 200 % return during a 5 year time period, averaging 40 % yearly return and with the high-risk you have even better returns during the 5 year period. You are able to see that the equity curve increased linearly which was also good, we did not experience any drawdowns.

What if we also included a safety net to prevent a total account wipe out? To execute the strategy I placed 5 pending orders and the last one was edited with a stop-loss order meaning above that level all open orders would have been closed. We saw a smaller profit but had an increase of 800% since 2010. You also see from the graph that we had some big drawdowns, for me this is a good strategy rather than adjusting another one to only make average money. I am comfortable with a certain amount of risk, but I would have not risked more than 10,000 USD if I wanted to do a live trade on this.

Summary

We see that if we wish to trade like the big banks then we need to throw out the stop-loss using mentality. When institutions are in a buy mode of a security they are *really* long and if the security goes down then they simply purchase more of it at a lower level. They will rarely if ever use a stop-loss. They operate without stops because they can. What smaller traders can risk is a margin call or a stop-out if the security never retraces. Traders when executing the strategy, after the short position is open, can consider using a stop-loss in addition to where you place sell limit orders. If the price increases even further you close all your orders and take the loss. If I were a passive investor I might prefer this technique than to always get stop hunted by the brokers and lose out on trades. This strategy could be considered, but preferably with low risk, small lot sizes and as part of a broader portfolio. Have a look at the steady growth of the equity curve, we never had a drawdown which is a good sign to make money as the big traders do.

Adding To Winners – How Professionals Manage Their Trades

As we have seen, the Martingale strategy is simply buying more if long, or selling more if short when the market goes against you. There is another strategy called the Anti-Martingale. To execute this you will double or triple your investment when you are in profit. In our scenario, you enter the market and are long a stock with an entry price of $50. You also have a predefined rule that if the market moves up to $55 you will move the stop-loss of the first trade to break-even and open another trade with double the lot size. Your target price for both trades will be $60.

The advantage of the strategy is that if you are correct you will make much more money than you lose when you are wrong. The market does not have to move so much, because you have increased your trading amount. This is known as "adding to the winners." The disadvantage is that if the market reverses after triggering you second or your fifth order, you are now trading with additional orders and will experience larger losses.

Scenario 1								
Trades	Amount		Price		SL		TP	Result
1		0.0100		1.5610		1.5600		1.5590	-10
Total									-10
Scenario 2								
Trades	Amount		Price		SL		TP	Result
1		0.0100		1.5610		1.5600		1.5590	0
2		0.0300		1.5600		1.5610		1.5590	-30
Total									-30
Scenario 3								
Trades	Amount		Price		SL		TP	Result
1		0.0100		1.5610		1.5600		1.5590	20
2		0.0300		1.5600		1.5610		1.5590	30
Total									50

Scenario 1: Only the first trade is triggered and stop-loss is activated if we have a loss of -10 USD.

Scenario 2: Both trades are triggered, but stop-loss of the first trade is changed to break-even, but if the stop-loss of the second is triggered we get a loss of -30 USD.

Scenario 3: Both trades are triggered, and both reaches take profit we get a total profit of 50 USD.

Entry Signal

If we have a high above Bollinger bands and the candle after it closes below the previous close, we open a short trade (see chart).

Trade Management

If the price goes above 100 pips we close the trade. If the market moves 100 pips below the entry price of the initial trade we open a second trade with double the amount of the first. We then change the stop-loss of the first trade to break-even. Stop-loss of the second trade is same as the entry price of the first trade, which is 100 pips. Both positions have take-profit at 200 pips from where we entered the first trade. We used a volatility-based distance, our distance between the orders is a function of the daily volatility. This is important because, as mentioned before, the volatility is different at different times.

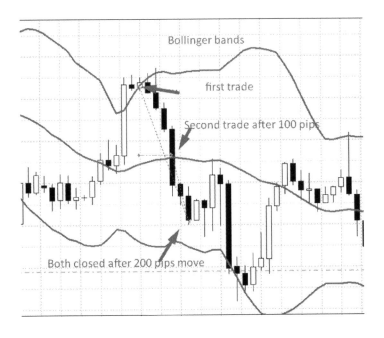

Graph above illustrates our entry signal and the trade management.

Test instrument: EURUSD
Test period: 01.01.2009 - 01.01.2016
Starting balance: 10,000 USD
Timeframe: 4 Hour chart

Test results:

Average profit	Sum profit	Winning trade	Total trades	Standard dev	Relnumber
27	8949	140	330	206	2

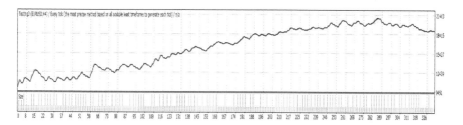

During a period of 7 years we had around 90% profit, of total 330 trades 140 were profitable trades. You see that the equity curve also increased steadily which is good, we had some losses and some wins, but on average we made money.

Summary

We can conclude that this trade management tool is a good way to deal with trades that do not have a good winning profile. One can also see from the equity curve that we did not experience any huge drawdowns. The key is that you must ensure that the distance between your orders are a function of volatility. This strategy should be considered if you are seeking an alternative to the traditional 1:2 or 1:3 risk to reward ratio. Many professional traders use this strategy with much success in their trades.

Conclusion

Thank you for making it through to the end of *Expert Advisor Programming and Advanced Forex Strategies*. Let's hope it was informative and that it was able to provide you with some additional tools that will help you achieve your trading goals. The next steps, as I always recommend in my books is to take action. Set up a demo account with your favorite trading provider and test the strategies until you achieve the results that you need to see before opening a live account.

Profile of the Author

Wayne Walker is the director of a global capital markets education and consulting firm (gcmsonline.info). He has several years experience in leading and coaching teams of Investment Advisors and has managed top performing teams in the Private Client Group based on Bench Mark Earnings (BME).

Printed in Great
Britain
by Amazon